When Religion Is Not Enough

EVERY

PLACE

IS HOLY

GROUND

Richard Venus

ISBN: 1461104491
ISBN-13: 9781461104490
Library of Congress Control Number: 2011906261
CreateSpace, North Charleston, SC

Preface

It was the middle of the winter semester when Richard appeared at my door bearing a draft of these collected sermons/reflections and inviting me to write the preface. I was delighted to be asked and eager to do so, but was rather pressed for time and unsure when I would be free to turn my attention to it.

It is summer now and I am grateful for Richard's patience because, even though this book is the fruit born of meditative jogging, it is not something to be read on the run. Instead, it is an inspiring collection that is meant to be appreciated leisurely, one thought-provoking theme at a time.

The chapters are short and each begins with an anecdote about either the poignant - a woman fleeing from her burning home, a Jew given hospitality in a Palestinian refugee camp, a friend with dementia, or the seemingly banal - feeling pain while bending over a laundry basket, sharing an umbrella, or the controversial - science versus religion, immigration, racism. Succinctly told, the stories trigger questions that give us pause - "Why is God always punishin' folks who are tryin'?"- and lead us into our depths, not for "answers" but for insights - "Healers are hosts who patiently and carefully listen to the story of the suffering stranger."

Exploring each theme is like entering a labyrinth; the path is winding with a surprising and illuminating juxtaposition of wisdom drawn from scientists, poets, journalists, feminists, mystics, activists, rabbis, ministers, pagans and Buddhists, to name a few. And like a labyrinth, the journey ultimately leads one to his or her own center. As the author explains, the journey involves taking risks, asking big questions, being aware of options, making ethical choices and accepting blunders, but always moving toward the center which is rooted in a self-knowledge and self-love that empowers individuals to care about others and world around them.

As a former journalist, interested in the pressing concerns of our times, the author understands the questions and concerns of those living in a secular, multi-cultural, globally engaged and politically divided landscape. As a Unitarian-Universalist minister, he agilely crisscrosses ethnic, gender, political, scientific and religious boundaries to gather the wisdom so sorely needed to inspire love, hope and a commitment to birthing a more just and caring world. In this collection, as in the leadership he has shown in the communities he has served, the author explores these themes with conviction, creativity and humor.

Bobby Kennedy often quoted the words of George Bernard Shaw: "some see things as they are and say why; I dream things that never were and ask why not." This book will appeal most to those who identify with the latter.

Dr. Judith Martin, ssj.

Acknowledgements

Chuck, David, Paul and Fred were four classmates at Union Theological Seminary in New York. We took turns preparing breakfast for each other. One week, as a religious education exercise, Chuck invited us to take turns building a "house" that would be descriptive of who we were. When it came for my turn, they described a cozy bungalow with a white picket fence, grassy green lawn upon which stood several flowering trees. A walkway led to a wide doorway that opened to a living room filled with a comfortable sofa and chairs. A kitchen was full of the smell of freshly brewed coffee and all about were open softly draped windows. There was one room, however, that was not finished: the library. This was their way of telling me I still had much to learn, and so it was. This book is written, in part, to say that I have listened to them, and while my library is still far from complete, I have worked on filling it. Their offered advice has guided me ever since. It is to them that I dedicate this book.

There are many others to whom I am indebted for guiding me through the many years of my spiritual journey. The congregation of the 14th Avenue United Methodist Church in Detroit taught me the real-world way of ministry. The members of three Unitarian Universalist churches I have served over the past 20 plus years have been kind, wise and generous in their support. Dr. Lois Henson came to my rescue during the time I was a candidate for the Miami Valley Unitarian Universalist Fellowship and has remained a trusted physician ever since. I regard the friendship of Rick and Hillary Wagner as truly life enriching. They introduced me and our congregation to a rich variety of music that deepened our spiritual understanding and made possible our worship. Rick has edited and made invaluable suggestions to this volume. Professor Judith Martin enlarged my spiritual vision to include insights from the world's religions. Trudy Krisher's support and advice was what I needed to complete this work.

Without my wife Marcia this book would never have been finished. She has offered love, support and wise counsel and to her I offer my deepest appreciation.

I have used others' words in my preaching and in this book. I have tried to credit those from whom I have borrowed. To those I give my thanks. To those whom I have used without credit I offer my apologies and please, if you recognized yourself in a quote, let me know so I may credit you in future volumes.

Introduction

I am a runner. I run in the morning with my dog. Come sun, rain, show, sleet or hail, I run. Sometimes I run in three or four of those conditions in one three to five mile stretch.

Skeptics say it must be boring. It's not. I come to hills and wonder how I got there. My mind has been elsewhere. I write letters to friends, make speeches I'd like to give, curse my enemies, wonder about the budget crisis, the war in Afghanistan, my granddaughter's homework and then I wave to passers-by.

No two days are the same. There are deer who look at me as intently as I stare at them. There are weeds to watch as they change color and shape with the seasons, and puddles to splash in. I saw a Great Blue Heron one misty morning rise up from her nest on the muddy Miami River.

Without my glasses, or sometimes with them in the rain, objects take on strange shapes. One holiday I said hello to an evergreened mailbox by the edge of a graveled driveway, mistaking it for a third-grader waiting for her school bus.

I wonder and reflect and question as I travel these hills and dales. These essays are, in part, a result of those traveling ruminations.

I wonder about things as I pass on those early morning runs. At the end of one lonely stretch, along the edge of a corn field, stands a grey-blue farm house with parts that go in and out, this way and that, suggesting it has had several reincarnations as the needs of the inhabitants have changed.

One morning, very early, as the sun was pinking up the grey sky behind the barn, I trotted by the front yard. I turned my head to see a woman draped in what I guessed to be a frayed light-blue terrycloth bathrobe. Her arms were folded across her chest. She was standing in the broad, dusty picture window staring out over the road to the empty weed-filled field in the distance. I wondered if she was the Diane whose name appeared with Bill's on the mailbox I passed as I continued up the road. I am not sure our eyes ever met. It didn't seem like she was connecting with anything outside herself in that moment.

I wondered about her for a few yards, then my dog was chased by a local cocker spaniel and my brain moved on to something else.

I still run down Bill and Diane's desolate road. I call it their road because theirs is the only name I find on that stretch, but changes have occurred and I wonder what they mean. Surrounded by "No Trespassing," "Travel at Your Own Risk," and "Trotters Riding Stables," signs, was the mailbox bearing their names. One day only Bill's name remained. Diane was smudged out with some off-white paint, probably left over from the living room ceiling.

Months have gone by and the sign has changed again. Bill's name is gone now. None has replaced it. Dogs still charge forth from the back yard to bark at my running mate. Someone or ones must occupy the place, although I never see them.

I think of the woman in the window as I trudge by and wonder if her thoughts that morning were about a fight she had with Bill earlier, or about a lover she could not tell him about, or him her, or just the day that lay ahead. I wonder what happed as I run by a place where two names have disappeared from view. I wonder if those two are sad about leaving the grey-blue farm.

I wonder about people when I run. I wonder what makes them come together and go apart. I wonder about life, and what makes sense and doesn't.

The essays in this book are some of the conclusions and questions that accompany me as I wonder and wander, trudging slowly ahead.

Table of Contents

The Importance of Blunder

One of the fundamental capacities of human beings is that we make mistakes. We get lost. We get confused. We do dumb things.

One of the tasks at my church in Detroit was to pick up several members who lived some distance away and bring them to the worship service. On one particular wintry Sunday morning I invited my daughter, who was perhaps three or four, to go with me. "I'll go get the car," I said to her. "You put on your snowsuit and I'll pick you up and take you with me." I then trudged out to the garage, got in the car, drove off, picked up the waiting church-goers and returned home to find my daughter waiting with her mother on the steps, still in her snow-suit hoping that I would take her with me. As I recall this story I can still see the sad look in her eyes and fell the ache in my heart for my very terrible mistake. Mistakes are the milestones on our journey toward understanding.

In his autobiography, Peter Fleck, who turned from a life in banking and finance to the ministry writes: "I wish that history would leave me alone. I mean my personal history. The things that have happened to me and the things that have not happened to me. The things I have done and the things I have left undone. I wish I could make my peace with these things. But I can't. Sometimes I lie awake at night, wishing I had done what I have not done, wishing I had left undone what I have done. And I realize that I missed opportunities for happiness because I didn't know that they existed; had I known, I would have seized them. I realize that I often neglected to experience life at any given moment, by itself and for itself and not as a stepping stone to something else."[1]

As the poet Robert Frost once said, education was "hanging around until you catch on."[2]

That's a thought worth remembering because as we have moved through history we have made choices we wish we could reverse, we have made decisions we wish we had not made, we have spoken words we wish we could take back both as individuals and as a church.

When we reflect on our past, I remind us that we have not made this journey without miscues. We have not listened when we should, we've ignored wisdom when it was offered, hurt others with our good intentions, and suffered hurt from those well-intentioned. Some voices we have not heard because we did not listen carefully to what their hearts were saying. Our journey has been a search to get it right amid missteps, false starts and wrong decisions.

Supreme Court Justice Oliver Wendell Holmes found himself unable to find his ticket as he boarded a train home. As he rummaged through his pockets and bags, he was recognized by the conductor who said, "Don't worry, Justice Holmes, you don't need a ticket. Just send it to us later when you find it." Quite irritated, the justice replied, "My dear sir, the problem is not 'Where is my ticket?' the problem is 'Where am I going?' "

Through eons and eons we humans have evolved out of the messy process of evolution, blundering our way. We are still struggling to catch on. No matter how egregious our errors, however, we rise each morning with a fresh day ahead. We are part of what is an original blessing, part of an experiment testing whether we humans can find ourselves at home on this planet, in this country, in this state, in this town, in some tiny space on some street on which we live.

The distinguished photographer Ansel Adams was also an accomplished pianist. At a party for friends he played Chopin's F Major Nocturne. "In some strange way," he writes, "my right hand started off in F-sharp major while my left hand behaved well in F-major. I could not bring them together. I went through the entire nocturne with my hands separated by a half-step." The next day he related how a fellow guest complimented him on his performance saying, "You never missed a wrong note."[3]

"Mistakes are at the very base of human thought," writes the biology writer Lewis Thomas in his book, <u>The Medusa and the Snail</u>. "If we were not provided with the knack of being wrong we could never get anything useful done. We think our way along by choosing between right and wrong alternatives, and the wrong choices have to be made as frequently as the right ones. We get along in life this way. We are built to make mistakes, coded for error."[4]

Dr. Thomas reminds us that all the progress in the world has evolved from the first DNA, that life-designing molecule in every cell. Today's entire DNA is simply an extension of that first molecule, but if human intelligence had had its way we would not have done it right. We would have made it to be perfect, it would not have occurred to us that the thing had to make mistakes.

"The capacity to blunder slightly," writes Dr. Thomas "is the real marvel of DNA. Without this special attribute, we would still be anaerobic bacteria, and there would be no music.... If scientists had set about to design such a similar replicating molecule, we would have found some way to correct this ability to make errors, and evolution would have been stopped in its tracks. What scientists would have worked toward is perfect DNA without the capacity to change or mutate. The result would be that all we would have is what we started with, and no Pterodactyls, robins, Homo sapiens, or Mozart."[5]

We are here by pure chance and mistake.

Michael Jordan is a nine-time All-Star, four-time MVP, two-time Olympic gold-medalist. On the basketball court he was the man who shackled gravity and made the impossible seem routine and the merely difficult look easy. Yet in an interview before he retired he said, "I've missed more than 9,000 shots in my career. I've lost more than 300 games. Twenty-six times I've been trusted to take the game winning shot and missed. I've failed over and over and over again in my life. And that is why I succeeded."[6]

It is significant that Jordan, perhaps the greatest basketball player ever, attributes his success to his failures. He admits he didn't get it right all the time, yet that does not keep him from acknowledging all that he brought to the world of sport. I commend Jordan's thoughts to our keeping. He reminds us that we succeed not simply in spite of our missteps, our failures, or mistakes, but because of them.

Churches, synagogues, mosques are filled with very human people whose very nature that makes them who they are, imperfect beings on a journey toward the good. It is a journey filled with heroism, nobility and grandeur, but also conflict, ignorance and injustice. It is a journey taken because most of us want to do what is right. I remind each of us, however, that in taking these steps we are moving in untried territory and we sometimes loose our way. We will be better for it if we accept our mistakes, learn from them and move on, without rancor, recrimination or self-doubt.

The Rev. Richard Gilbert writes, "I am sustained by a faith in a feeling that I belong here, that I have a right to be here, that perfection is not in the cards, nor need it be, that striving for simple humanity is more important than seeking sainthood.

And that faith remains to sustain me no matter what happens in the everyday as I seek to find out where it is I am going."[7]

Our mistakes must inform us, but we cannot be stuck in the past by our missteps or our successes. The future of liberal religious faith lies in the ability to define the religious and spiritual dimensions of the ecological crisis confronting the world, the willful imposition of violence upon those with whom we disagree, and the abhorrent treatment of women and children throughout third world countries. There is a need for a new religious vision in which every place is holy ground, all people are sacred and all of us are embarked on the same journey. We can no longer be defined by the traditions out of which we emerged or in which we are stuck out of fear of making mistakes.

At the heart of wisdom is the belief that violence as a weapon of nation-building is wrong. That men are superior to women is another woefully destructive idea, while social policy based on profit-taking is short-sighted. It is the celebration of the worth and dignity of every human being that is the beginning point of any wholesome ethic and the building of a caring community is as good a starting place as any.

In so doing we must take ourselves seriously. We must be those who are creating a kind of spirituality that fits the twenty-first century by the very living of that wholesome ethic we espouse. We are called to say who we are and what we believe and why that message is vital to our generation amid the community we serve.

Creating a world out of the darkness in which we now find ourselves can only begin were we are, in tiny places and in spite of our missteps, but holding out the hope that our voices will be heard.

I realize such a charge reflects a naiveté and optimism that flies in the face of much of what we see and experience every day, but it may be the only vision that will make possible the good that we seek.

Questions for further reflection

1. Have there been mistakes in your past that have shaped your life? If so, what were they?
2. If there is one mistake you have made you wish you could take back, what is it?

Religion Is Not Enough

Religion is not enough. Religious faith, spirituality, a sense of the holy, or any spiritual path cannot completely or fully explain death or life. Nor can philosophy, biology, memorial services, or studies of the Koran, the Book of Genesis, or the Buddha fully answer the questions that life brings. Wherever one goes to find the ultimate truths with which life challenges us, the search ends with more questions than answers.

I was sure I had or would soon find the answers, until a number of years ago, in the middle of the night, I was called to the front door of my house in inner-city Detroit by the pounding of Mrs. Pac, a Caucasian, single mom on welfare who was a teacher in my church's children's education program. This slender wisp of a woman was covered with soot and hanging on the arm of her neighbor. Before I could speak or invite her in, she pointed her finger at me and said, "Reverend Venus, why is God always punishin' folks who are tryin'?"

She didn't open with "Hello," or "Could I come in?" All she wanted was an answer to this fundamental question about suffering and pain. I looked up the street where I saw fire trucks with firemen pouring water on flames shooting from her house. Later, I learned that five of her seven children had burned to death in that fire.

I have lived many years since Mrs. Pac came to my door. I have received degrees in counseling and guidance and theology. I have worked as a minister, therapist, journalist, and carpenter, but neither then nor now do I have a satisfactory answer for her question or many others that the harshness of life presents. Hers is a question that haunts me to this day. After Mrs. Pac's story made the TV news, several viewers called me to suggest that I "just tell her that God wanted her children to be with him in heaven." Others said the loss of her children was part of a larger plan that only God understood. Such responses did not satisfy me then, and, while volumes have been written on the subject of evil, suffering and death, to this day I still find no satisfactory way to understand her question. It is an ultimate question that defies a conclusive answer.

Some argue that God has chosen to limit his power to give us freedom to choose, therefore bad things happen. To them I ask: What good is God, if he or she or it doesn't stop such evil? Why did the "Ultimate Power in the universe" not intervene over against the Nazis at the death camps of Buchenwald or Treblinka or the mass torture and killings in Serbia or Rowanda unless he was powerless to do so? If he could have intervened and didn't, how can we say there is an all-loving deity who has any power over our lives?"

Some suggest God did intervene through those who survived. Those who gave of themselves so others might live or who went on to live good lives after their experiences make meaningful the sacrifice of others. I can appreciate how this then asks of each of us to make good visible in the world, but are those who intervene with good works making God unnecessary or irrelevant? If such intervention is present where so much evil continues to abound, isn't that an extreme way for a supreme being to guide the world? I can understand why an all-powerful deity might leave us to our own devices in order for us to grow and mature in ways of love and caring. If we have been left to our own devices, however, what good is such a God to us now?

Others might argue that we mere humans cannot know the plans, purposes, love, and will of God. It is enough to believe that he is beyond our understanding and therefore we simply live by faith. If so, then I ask what good is my mind with which this creator endowed me if ultimate answers are beyond my intellect?

My friend Rick Wagner has deeply studied the world's religions and notes, "Buddha believes that the existence of a creator is something we will never be able to determine in our lives; therefore, live life with goodness and compassion—if there is a creator, that creator would have wanted you to do no less than that. If there is not a creator, then you still have contributed to making the world a better place.

Ultimately, to live with goodness and compassion, whether there be a creator God or not, is timely and truthful wisdom that is beyond the confines of church or synagogue or mosque.

Religious responses to Mrs. Pac and others who struggle with the problem of evil, suffering, injustice, and the mysteries life presents to us all are inadequate at best, for we can never completely understand or define the ultimate nature of existence. I admit these attempts at defining the spiritual nature of our lives are only attempts to offer pictures of how we might live amid the questions, rather than provide final answers.

Several years ago, Vincent Canby, a movie reviewer for *the New York Times*, described waiting for the subway train under 42nd Street and Broadway in New York City. As secretaries, school children, bankers, physicians, and the usual assortment of commuters began squeezing their way past each other and into the waiting train cars, a young man in a torn jean jacket and muddy, frayed blue jeans pointed his finger at a properly kept gentleman in a white shirt, striped tie, and blue suit and shouted, "Hey mister, give me back my yo-yo!"

The well-dressed gentleman looked back with a somewhat bemused and puzzled look. The finger-pointer kept it up. "Hey, mister, give me back my yo-yo!" at which point the doors of the train began to shut, but because this accuser stood between them the train could not move. Instead, they just banged against his shoulders as he continued to accuse the man in the blue suit of the theft of his yo-yo.

Finally, a burly commuter, perhaps an off-duty steamfitter, squeezed through the crowded train car, grabbed the young man by the shoulders, picked him up and set him down on the platform. The doors then closed and the train, including Canby and the man in the blue suit, pulled away from the station.

About then the rider in the blue suit reached in his pocket and pulled out a round, red object that obviously was a yo-yo. The passengers shuffled about, staring in disbelief. "Oh, my God," exclaimed one passenger. "He does have the yo-yo."

When Canby got off at the next stop he looked around to see where the movie cameras were hidden, for surely this was a made-up play amid real life extras. There were no hidden lenses of any kind, no directors plotting the action. This was real life for which Canby could only stand in wonder.

So it is with life. It is filled with mystery, humor, grief, heroics, vengeance, cruelty, and love. Religion seeks to help us live amid all these puzzles and problems and promises. In the name of religious beliefs, some have given even their lives to make their messages of hope present among us. I commend to you Jesus of Nazareth, Gautama Buddha, Mohandas Gandhi, Susan B. Anthony, Ralph Waldo Emerson, Sojourner Truth, Martin Luther King, Jr., Nelson Mandela, Dorothy Day, and Margaret Sanger, all who have given witness to the truth. These and many others have struggled on behalf of religious questions, either within the institutions of religion or by living the truths that religion seeks to hold. The truths they lived can guide us, It is up to us to decide what their truth is for ourselves as we continue our life's journey.

Questions for further reflection

1. What would you have said to Mrs. Pac if she had come to your door with such a question?
2. Name those who you find helpful guides to your life. Are they religious figures, or secular? Does that make a difference?

Dare to Love the World

I want to tell you of two of my recent experiences. The first happened in Kroger's, while I was waiting in the checkout lane. The woman in front of me had unloaded her basket. As she was writing out her check, she shouted at the cashier in a way most all of us could hear, saying, "Why is it that when I come here, you never have what I need? The reason I shop early in the morning is because I'm very busy and this is the only time I have. I don't know why you don't have lunch meat, I mean, lunch meat should be so basic." The cashier looked puzzled, wondering what it was about lunch meat that she could fix, but then asked about the kind of lunch meat the woman was looking for. "Kroger's, you know, your own. You know, turkey and ham! Why can't you have it?"

"I'm sorry," the cashier said, "I will mention it to the manager." But the woman continued to shout. "That is why I will shop somewhere else. I just don't understand why you can't have lunch meat here."

A few months ago, during rush hour, I was waiting my turn in traffic at the corner of Mad River and Alex Bell roads, which is a few miles from my home. As is often the case in that time of day, the line of cars is long in all four directions as each driver waits for his or her turn through the four-way stop. As I approached the intersection, I waited for the other cars to take their turn. When I thought it was my turn, I started out, but just as I did a shiny black sedan pulled into the intersection as well. I quickly put on my brakes. As the other driver crossed in front of me he turned his head and gave me a look. It was not a look that said, "Gee, isn't this a tricky corner, and isn't it amazing that we find ways to regulate traffic without a light?" Rather it was a look spoken down his nose that said, "Buddy, how dare you. Don't even think about coming into my path."

There have been times when I have given someone a dirty look, been rude or impatient over some unintentional mistake. I suspect we have all experienced from others the disrespectful behavior that seems to be creeping more and more into our daily lives: sales clerks who couldn't care less about service, drivers who think neighborhood streets are miniature race courses, service people who believe you are the problem when asking to return a faulty appliance.

About now you are probably saying to yourselves, "Oh, how silly, these are the petty irritations in life, don't get so worked up. Consider for a moment the events in Tucson, Arizona: the shooting of Congresswoman Gabrielle Giffords; the killing of her aide Gabriel Zimmerman (30),; Judge John Roll, chief judge of the U.S. District Court for Arizona; nine-year old Christina-Taylor Green; Dorothy "Dot" Morris (76); homemaker Phyllis Schneck (79); Dorwan Stoddard (76), retired construction worker, whose wife Mavy was wounded, along with eighteen others in a senseless shooting at a shopping mall.

In light of events like the one in Tucson, my question is whether the somewhat minor irritations I noted earlier reflect a larger malaise. Is our insensitivity to those around us reflected in the shrill discourse we regularly hear over issues of affirmative action, abortion, gay rights, privatization of Medicare, and many of the pressing social issues of the day? Do the steady minor irritations we too routinely experience contribute to a murderous sociopath? I wonder if our way of handling these issues of everyday irritations and those of major social importance are somehow related.

In this time when we have experienced how far beyond these slights we go in the direction of violence against others, why what is currently described as a decline in civility more and more with us and what might we do about it?

This decline is certainly not a new phenomenon. In the eighteenth century, the signer of the Declaration of Independence, Benjamin Rush, complained that the "principles and morals" of the people had declined. It was also a time when etiquette books were all the rage. The Ms. Manners of those days were advising dinner guests to discontinue their practice of wiping their teeth on the tablecloth after dinner. I am not talking about table manners, but how we treat one another.

A code of civility did emerge among us, and some have suggested that because consideration of others was a necessary part of fostering good work habits and social interaction, concern for proper behavior created a middle-class that grew at a surprising rate following the Civil War. Being polite and courteous has only little to do with using the right fork, however, and much more with instilling a sense of concern and regard for others.

I remember in one of the first books on etiquette I read as a teenager, the overriding principle of the author was a reminder that if I couldn't remember which spoon to use, being respectful of one's host would be even more appropriate and would override any social *faux pas.*

Of course, Freud and others have long held that a polite demeanor is actually a thin veneer hiding the raw forces of lust, greed, and fear that lie just below the surface of such superficial behavior. What we have seen in recent years is violence becoming the primary way to resolve differences. But whether or not we have made gains over time in our behavior or are simply reverting to our primal selves, I sense there is a rising lack of respect among people, and we are less caring of one another than is good for us.[8]

Many have pointed out that our whole social order is in transition. The values of yesterday are not holding and the values of tomorrow are not yet universal. As one newspaper report reminds us, "The average consumer holds more computer power in his or her pocket than existed in the entire world thirty years ago." In this transition time, roles are shifting and the sense of knowing who we are and finding a comfortable niche into which to fit our lives is evaporating.

There is also a growing demand for recognition and a place in the human family by those who were once marginalized. Such changes are long overdue and necessary, but they produce a heightened insecurity among many who are not comfortable or feel threatened by these changes.

Following 9/11, it has become clear that enemies of the United States are many and determined. There are those who agree with the filmmaker turned children's book author, Spike Lee, who, following the massacre in Tucson, suggested that the United States has become the most violent nation on earth. In a recent *New York Times* collection of articles about gun control, I was amazed to read the number of writers suggesting that the Tucson killings call for all of us to carry firepower on our belts.

There is also the sense that those in power are calling upon the "everyone does it" defense for behavior that is clearly without honor, if not illegal. Those we have entrusted with power regularly abuse that trust. Many in high places have eroded our confidence in the integrity of government. There is a growing uneasiness that those we have elected will honorably represent us. We live knowing that an increasing number in elected office have bought their way in and come with flawed character.

At the same time, the religious systems of the past—through which we have defined ourselves, from which we have derived the values by which we lived, and in which we have found the very meaning that made sense out of our lives—those belief systems are today wobbling and losing power. The truths held out by religious institutions are less self evident and there is no longer a church or synagogue or mosque that can serve as the compelling authority it once was. The religious fundamentalist movement in this country based on blessing the nation is growing not only in the U.S. but around the world, while rarely standing against its excesses and wrongdoing. It offers no serious explanations for the complex nature of life and the myriad of problems besetting humankind.

The world that is fast transforming itself has eroded our confidence in traditional values and the traditional definitions of right and wrong. It may well be that the anger, violence, and incivility we offer one another may reflect a spiritual crisis that lies at the heart of modern life.

There are reasons for the anger and incivility we experience. We look about and see that the once secure ports in life, including church, workplace, and home, no longer are the safe havens, or at least not familiar ones, they once were. Workers who once could count on yearly raises and lifetime security have found wages barely, if at all, keeping up with inflation. In many cases they find they are falling farther and farther behind, with their children wondering what will happen to their future. Job security has been replaced by downsizing. Two income households are necessary to keep the bills paid, and fewer and fewer workers are doing more and more. *The New York Times* recently reported that we have not yet seen the bottom of the number of foreclosures and many more lie ahead.

All the while, we see a growing gap between rich and poor. Basic benefits, such as health care and pensions, are becoming less affordable or even possible, while superstars in finance, management, sports, and entertainment call down huge salaries and have lifestyles most of us never even dream about. Some in Washington decry efforts to bring at least a minimum of health care to those without. I wonder whether the growing divide between the super-rich superstars of television, movie, sports, and junk bonds and the rest of us contributes to the loss of self-worth or importance?

The early twentieth century psychoanalyst Alfred Adler suggested that our human behavior stems largely from our sense of being somewhat less than others. He wrote: "The greater the sense of inferiority that has been experienced, the more powerful is the urge for conquest and the more violent the emotional agitation." If he is even partly right, he helps explain why some react in anger over the loss of a sense of importance and worth endemic to a society that frequently begins decision-making with the financial bottom line, not human enrichment.

Another underlying reason for this decline, which is more pervasive and fundamental than the rest, is described by Garry Wills in a recent article in the *New York Review of Books*.[9] Why, Wills asks, has John Wayne often been chosen as American's number one movie star? Because, he argues, our hero is the frontiersman. To become urban or suburban is to break our human spirit. Freedom is out on the plains, under an endless sky. A pent-in American ceases to be American, a theme described early on by Ralph Waldo Emerson. In a lecture entitled "Young Americans," Emerson argued that Americans needed the boundless West in order to become themselves.

Our intense love of the rights of the individual as expressed by Emerson and many thereafter is exemplified in the practice of going off by yourself to be saved. John Wayne embodied that spirit; free to roam, untrammeled, unspoiled, breathing a larger air than those crammed behind desks and on busy streets. He is the hero who combines all the mythic ideas about American individualism--contact with nature, distrust of government, dignity achieved by performance, skepticism of experts. As Wills adds, "Just as one had to go off alone to be saved, Americans have always felt that reality will be encountered and spiritual growth will occur when we go out from society's constrictions toward cleansing solitude, toward nature—toward Walden."[10]

I sense that it is this reliance on the importance of the individual, as fiercely promoted by Glen Beck, Rush Limbaugh, and a host of public officials, while important also leads to incivility. Lily Tomlin once quipped, "We're all in this alone." She's wrong, but many believe it, and many live like it. Many do not feel connected in any real sense to those other than immediate family and friends, and often those connections are too easily broken.

To be connected is to have one's freedom limited by another and to be responsible for one's behavior because it affects another. Maybe you and I would rather be freer than that, we'd rather celebrate our freedom than give in to compromise. So when I bump up against you at a grocery counter or a traffic stop, I am free to shout in your face or look down my nose because we have no connection. If I believe my country right or wrong, I am free to go to war to prove it or carry a gun to back me up.

While there may be good reasons for the anger, the fear, the shrill voices, the decline in civility, there are still far more who refuse to give in, who regularly volunteer their services on behalf of others, who contribute liberally to the general welfare, who honestly and dutifully carry out their elected positions, who seek to get the best for their employees. Every day customers at Kroger's say they appreciate the incredible bounty that is available, and my experience has been that the clerks are most helpful. Many at that corner of Mad River and Alex Bell politely wait their turn and allow others to pass without the slightest hint of hostility and often a useful wave of the hand to offer direction.

While rightly honoring individual self-discovery, it is worthy to proclaim that we are connected to each other and to the earth. Truth and meaning in our lives is found not in the search for the open frontier, but here in the midst of the real world, the everyday, where we mix it up together and when we listen to, speak with, and honor each other, living with the tension of being unique individuals who are part of a community of seekers on a religious journey.

The writer Mary Oliver says it well when she notes: "There is only one question, 'How do we love the world?'" That, for me, is the question for us. It asks how are we to be with each other on this planet, and specifically, with those we know, as well as the stranger among us.

In a recent column in the *New York Times*, David Brooks reflects on President Obama's speech in Tucson following those shooting deaths I noted earlier. Mr. Brooks reports that the President didn't try to explain the rampage that occurred there, but noted our sense of loss. He also celebrated the lives of the victims and the possibility for renewal. The columnist goes on to note that even a great speech will not usher in a period of civility, because we are flawed human beings and we will slip back into failure, weakness, and ignorance. "Even if you are at your best," Mr. Brooks writes, "your efforts will be laced with failure. The truth is fragmentary and it's impossible to capture all of it. ...The world is more complicated than any human intelligence can comprehend. ...Each of [our] efforts may also be flawed, <u>but together, if the system is working well, they move things gradually forward</u>."[11] (*emphasis mine*)

If we dare to love the world, we will have to face head on the violence and the tenderness, the arrogance and the humility, the pain and the joy, the changes and the opportunities. If we dare to love the world, as Mr. Brooks puts it, *together* we will move things gradually forward.

Writer Nancy Mairs, who is confined to a wheelchair with multiple sclerosis, notes: "The charity that begins at home cannot rest there but draws one inexorably over the threshold and off the porch and down the street and so out and out and out and out into the world which becomes the home wherein charity begins until it becomes possible, in theory at least, to love the whole of creation with the same patience, affection, and amusement one first practiced in between the pouts and tantrums, with parents, siblings, partner, and children."

Our lives are connected, and that is why we talk about a community for all of us—because we care for each other, through simple gestures of kindness, letting someone into traffic, saying thank you and I'm sorry, listening instead of interrupting, healing the wounds, listening to the hurt, celebrating the joys. In seeing ourselves as connected, we will be more than civil. We will grow in compassion and caring. Perhaps, we will even make the world a little better place for all.

Questions for further reflection

1. Do you agree with Spike Lee that the U.S. is the most violent nation on earth? Why or why not?
2. Garry Wills asserts that many believe to become urban or suburban is to break our human spirit. Freedom is out on the plains, under an endless sky. A pent-in American ceases to be American. Do you agree?
3. "Even if you are at your best," writes *NY Times* columnist David Brooks, "your efforts will be laced with failure. The truth is fragmentary and it's impossible to capture all of it." Is failure a necessary part of life?

A Coin in the Beggar's Cup

As he routinely did, a man with no legs, using his arms and wheelboard, propelled himself through New York's Lexington Avenue subway while holding out a bent tin cup for donations. In the same IRT car was Susan Jacoby, a reporter for the *New York Times* who was in the midst of writing a story about charitable giving. She interviewed a number of people who saw this beggar. She asked them whether or not they had chosen to drop something in the man's cup and why. As you might imagine, the responses were varied.

"Why did I give?" asked a thirty-year-old paralegal assistant. "Honey, the man had *no legs*."

A man in a pinstripe suit sitting next to her put a coin in the cup. "When I saw you give, I was ashamed not to. As a rule," he went on, "I don't give to beggars. I don't know how the money is going to be used. Is he going to buy something to eat or buy a beer?"

Across the aisle, a woman overheard the conversation, rolled her eyes and cut in. "What, should the guy save your quarter to buy an artificial leg?"

A forty-ish man said: "I don't want you to think I'm stingy, because I give plenty of money to charity. But this giving to one individual, as sad as his situation is, just isn't effective, cost-effective. You know what I'm saying?"

A twenty-eight-year-old elementary schoolteacher said her husband would be furious with her for giving. "Once I started to give to a woman on the streets," she recalled, "and he stopped me by grabbing my arm. 'You can see that the woman's a druggie,' he said. For all I know, the man with no legs was a druggie, too. But he could buy a hamburger or some fries."

An electrician said, "What if one of my kids saw me not give to a man with no legs?"

"Women get that touchy-feely glow from giving to the homeless, don't they?" said another teacher. "There are government programs for people with real disabilities so he's cruising subways with another agenda. I don't want to insult you, but you must be stupid."

Another non-giver, a fifty-year-old declared: "That's not my responsibility. I pay plenty of taxes to take care of people like that."

A twenty-two-year-old college student said she gave not because she thought her fifty cents would help the beggar but because, she said, "I want to be able to look at myself in the mirror."[12]

Why do we give or not give to a beggar on a subway, or to the local art institute, or the St. Joseph's Homeless Shelter, or public radio, or church, synagogue, mosque, or any favorite charity you might care to name? What is it that guides our decisions about our money? Our reasons may be as varied as those people on that subway car.

I'm a soft touch, many would say. I give to beggars. I give to those with tin cups who ask, unless I am positive that they are going to use the money in a way I deem harmful. Most times I'm like the elementary school teacher on the train. I don't know if the beggar is a druggie, if he's going to buy a beer, or a burger, but it is clear to me that whatever the case, the person is in need.

Many argue that such assistance does more harm than good. By helping the beggar maintain his dependency on handouts, we contribute to his continuing poverty and low self-esteem. As another observer on that subway car said, "If people have to give to beggars to make themselves feel better about the suffering in the world, let them. It's much better to give to some organization that helps the disabled."

It is certainly common, and perhaps expected, to hear injunctions and invocations that we ought to do good with our money, that there is more to life than money, that money may not be the root of all evil, but certainly close to it, and the love of money, not money itself is the problem. These oft-repeated phrases are well-taken and perhaps to some extent even true, but they are heard so often that they have a "ho-hum" ring to them. They are ho-hum, in part, because they have been around for generations—from Benjamin Franklin to the preachers of the eighteenth century who admonished their flocks not to pursue money as an end, but to pursue that which was in keeping with the will of God. Years ago, Henry David Thoreau wrote, "Most of the luxuries, and many of the so-called comforts of life, are not only not indispensable, but positive hindrances to the elevation of mankind."

Over subsequent generations, however, economic theorists took those statements of the preachers and naturalists and turned them on their heads. Love of money was not the root of evil, they said, but rather it was the natural order of things for people to seek money.

Their central assumption suggested that the human spirit is characterized by an unrestrained drive for the accumulation of wealth, even beyond what is necessary for the immediate gratification of needs.[13] One's pursuit of wealth was now morally justified. If you were financially successful, it was because you worked hard and you deserved to get what you worked hard for. More to the point, it was in humanity's best interests for as many as possible to rise up the financial ladder.

Today we are perhaps more private about how much we earn and spend than we are about our sex lives. Money is a personal matter, yet how we spend money and why we spend it the way we do says much about who we are and what we believe. Many if not all of the moral choices we make are based on economics. Our culture and our personal lives are driven to various degrees by choices about how we spend our money.

Like several of those subway riders, there are those who argue that the marketplace ought to decide. Price and the market will ultimately determine the best choices for the greater good. If business and government allow the market to expand at a reasonable rate, money will eventually be distributed to those at all places on the economic spectrum. If those with wealth are allowed to invest and spend, their money would improve business conditions, which in turn would create more jobs and more opportunities for more and more people. This argument is summed up by the phrase we've often heard, that "the rising tide lifts all boats."

Another way of thinking is reflected in the subway rider who argued that he pays plenty of taxes and that is the best way to help. Government or the state ought to decide how money is distributed because it can allocate resources to those who are left out of the marketplace, to institutions and organizations where profits are not earned.

While we wrestle with how our money ought to be spent, we find ourselves besieged by private and personal needs to put food on the table, a roof over our heads, education, and health-care for ourselves or children, and all those things needed to make ends meet. At the same time we see the pressing needs of symphony orchestras, public radio, pregnant teens, cancer research, and homeless beggars on the street.

The choices are complex, but how we choose to use our money is a moral decision, a decision about what we value. How we spend our money may be one of the most direct expressions of what we most believe.

I know people who have made a job or career change that offered less money than another possible choice. Although the money was essential, their values caused them to make the choice for less money, suggesting that there are moral reasons for doing what we do that go beyond the economic bottom line. We make decisions that say we require more of ourselves and that others need more from us than can be decided only by profit motives. It may be as Robert Wuthnow has suggested in his book, *Poor Richard's Principle*. We choose to live our lives, he says, in ways that "give legitimate account of ourselves."[14] We give account of ourselves by being involved in how our money is used, how others use resources, how banks make loans, how governments dole out our taxes. It seems to me that our concern and our involvement is a matter of justice.

The marketplace is efficient, and I know that often money invested is wisely distributed and a growing economy can improve the lives of many who otherwise would be left poor and in need. I also know that if I let the market decide how money is to be spent, I miss an opportunity to decide what the money will be used for. I also assume that people are inspired not only to strive for more wealth, but also by a better nature than self-interest. I assume that goodness and generosity are also natural to the human spirit, and that the profit motive is not enough to satisfy our deepest hunger for justice.

A thirty-eight-year-old corporate lawyer who gave to that beggar on the subway said, "I don't think I'm a better person than anyone else because I sometimes give to beggars. I just can't, well, close my eyes all the time—the way we all do most of the time."

My understanding of why we put a coin in the beggar's cup comes from something someone said to me: "We do for others because others did for us."

We have a responsibility to do more than what is expedient or profit making because others made life possible for us in ways that for them went beyond the economic bottom line. They took risks; they held out their hand; they cried with those in need; they made sacrifices so schools and symphonies and safe houses could happen—sometimes for personal gain, sometimes not. They crossed oceans and sheltered the homeless. They rescued the immigrant; they searched for the lost; they took on the town bully so others might be safe or satisfied.

We would not be here but for those who reached down and carried themselves and their babies and strangers over mountains and rough plains, who made a softer bed for those who needed rest, who searched for cures to that which caused disease and pain. We give because we know that respect for the connected nature of all humanity is true. We know that we are here because others gave of themselves and those decisions were not simply market driven. Sometimes they made no economic sense, not in the short-term profit-loss column anyway. Therefore, we too give so there will be a future for those we do not even know.

"Let me make it simple," writes the Rev. Dr. Forrest Church in his book, *Life Lines*.[15] "For us to be here more than a billion billion accidents took place. All our ancestors lived to puberty, coupled, and gave birth. Not just our parents, grandparents, and great-grandparents. Take it all the way back to the beginning, beyond the first *Homo sapiens* to the *ur-paramecium*. Even the one in a million sperm's connection to the egg is nothing compared to everything else that happened from the beginning of time until now to make it possible for us to be here."

Against unimaginable odds, we have been given something we didn't deserve at all—the gift of life.

How does this affect the way we treat others? It means we will act toward others as being as unpredictable and amazing as we are. From earliest time, Dr. Church continues, "They too have run a billion billion gauntlets, emerging against almost impossible odds to walk here beside us on this planet. They are more than neighbors, they are kin, honest to God and hope to die kin."[16]

One of our wisest teachers advises us to love our neighbor as our self; even love our enemy. "He means, love our brother, even if he doesn't know he is our brother, and love our sister even if she doesn't know she is our sister. ...Somewhere they and we share one common ancestor who, with twenty-twenty hindsight, would do the same for us if she were here."[17]

I find it hard to comprehend or understand the vast reach back into time and history to include my ancestors, but I need to be reminded of the history that has created me and my world, and that my connections to others are long and great. Without their sacrifice I would not be here.

I have been given the gift of life. That life is sustained because those who came before me gave of their time, talent, money, even their lives, so the future might happen. I decide how I want that future to turn out, in part, by how I spend my money, just as society determines our future by its collective choices. That is why allowing the marketplace to decide is not enough. We create the kind of future we want by the way we use our resources. "It's like the creation of the coral reef," a friend once suggested to me, "which happens gradually, over long periods of time."

At a more immediate level, in our house, my wife is the bookkeeper. She pays the bills and keeps track of our money with some incredibly complex budget system for which I am grateful and by which I am mystified, but which also means that at times I have to ask her for money for a favorite cause. Recently, Planned Parenthood was holding a major capital fund drive. People were asked to make a significant donation. I asked and my wife initially frowned. "It's not in the budget," she said. In the ensuing days, however, as the deadline for contributions arrived, she agreed that we should give.

Only later she said she realized how important that gift was, not simply for what it gave to this non-profit organization, but what it gave to us.

"I have always been deeply grateful that women can have reproductive choice," she said. "After I thought about that, I realized that my money was going for more than just an organization. It was helping me understand where my values were. Now, where I spent my money said a great deal about what I believed in, and by having to decide where to give my money I got clearer who I was and what I stood for."

Economic justice is what we create as we remember our past and plan for our future. "Even small doses of morally principled behavior can count for a great deal," writes sociologist Wuthnow. "They become emblematic, serving to remind others that there are indeed higher values than they may have considered during a particular day at work or in the marketplace."[18]

What we do with our money, even in small doses, makes for economic justice. A market system makes money, and I am glad it does. We bend that system toward justice by how we decide to give of our money and ourselves. In our giving, we discover who we are.

Questions for further reflection

1. What is your response to someone asking for help? Would you give to the subway beggar with no legs? Do you give to those who ask, or do you prefer a more systematic way of assistance, as with social service agencies?
2. What are the guidelines you use in your charitable giving?
3. Identify two ways you recently gave money and the beliefs that were the basis of that giving?

To Whom It May Concern: The Nature of Prayer

Recently two friends were having a theological discussion. One said, "We Christians are so badly educated when it comes to the Bible.

"We are not," the other replied.

"Oh yeah?" said the first. "I'll bet you can't even recite the Lord's Prayer."

Each one slammed a five-dollar bill on the table and the second one said, "Now I lay me down to sleep, / I pray the Lord my soul to keep. / If I should die before I wake, / I pray the Lord my soul to take."

"Okay, okay," said the first. "You win."

It is well known that we have our questions and our doubts about the Bible, religion and life, and nowhere is that more apparent than when we address our prayers with, "To whom it may concern."

Maybe that's not as funny as it first sounds. We might ask, to whom do we offer our prayers? Are they offered to anyone at all, or are they a means to hear the voice within ourselves? Are they about petitioning a deity at all?

About prayer, I am puzzled. This Earth is but one planet in one solar system in one galaxy. We who pray are dwarfed by the vastness of the space beyond ourselves, and we no longer have the simple confidence that it was all created so that we ourselves might exist. Stars spin in distant space and explode, perhaps become gravity so dense that even light cannot escape its black hole force. There seems to be an ever-expanding cosmos. How are we to consider ourselves a privileged center in a universe now seen to be so complex that it no longer has a center? To whom do we address our prayers in such vast space and time? Where is God or the Creator? Inside this, outside, nowhere?

Once we thought the Earth was a stage set for the drama of ourselves; now we know that millennia of actors played this stage before us, and perhaps millennia of actors will succeed us. Neither are we the center of this play, nor is our particular religious story the center of religious history. Millions and millions of people pray. Who are we to believe our particular prayers are heard? The image of a God over whom all this vastness resides listening to the prayer of this insignificant speck of dust is difficult to appreciate or comprehend.

Prayer is one of those words with which we sometimes find ourselves uncomfortable, in part because of the baggage it carries. The notion that any one of us can call upon a God to do our bidding, do good for our side and not the other guys, or turn the storm away from our house but not to worry about our neighbor's house seems incredibly self-centered and ignores the very nature of that being to whom we are addressing these petitions.

In an article about prayer that recently appeared in my local newspaper, the *Dayton Daily News*, researchers reported that heart surgery patients "showed no benefit when strangers prayed for their recovery. And patients who knew they were being prayed for had a slightly higher rate of complications."[19] However, a cardiologist responded to this report saying he would rather put his faith in prayer than in a study that questioned its effectiveness. "Prayer has been time tested no matter what faith you belong to," he said.[20]

Given these questions and the reactions offered by this study, I have come to understand that prayer may be more universal than we might have at first believed. I begin with the notion that life is holy, that the spiritual is at the core of life, and that life is a mystery far beyond our wildest imagination.

A few thousand years ago, a writer or poet we know as the Psalmist stood on a hillside, peered into the dark night, and saw a zillion points of light. There were no city lights near that hillside to dim her vision of that night sky—it was as it is for us when we are on vacation tenting on a lakeshore and see the night sky for the first time. Led by the awesome night sky she exclaimed, "O Lord, how magnificent is thy place and what is man or woman that you are mindful of them." (Slight revisions in language are mine.)[21]

We stand not in the middle of that universe the Psalmist saw, but we stand on some pale blue dot somewhere in a vast universe surrounded by more points of light than we can possibly ever count or see or imagine, but we now peer into that vast space with Hubble, or on Mount Palomar, or with binoculars and telescopes, and we are in awe of the mystery, the wonder of life. We ask who are we on this tiny dot and we gasp, stutter, and mumble at the inscrutability of it all.

I know that in a particle accelerator somewhere in Massachusetts we smash atoms into nickel plates and we discover that the very stuff we stand on is made of the tiniest bits of matter that has more space than stuff. The very nature of us in the subatomic world of our existence confronts us and we stand in awe of the mystery and wonder of it all.

In a birthing room in any hospital, a mother opens her body and a newborn child sucks its first breaths, lets out a cry of welcome, and that mother, father, and those in attendance stand in awe and wonder of the beauty of it all.

Mathematicians and biochemists and new age physicists can give us formulas and principles and reasons why all this creation is with us and among us and before us, but even as they tell us why, the awe and wonder only increase. The more we understand, the more we don't understand; the more we know, the more we wonder.

Life is a miracle on this pale blue dot in the midst of a universe so vast we don't know if it's expanding or curving or just dying out. We are warmed by a ball of fire around which astronauts spin at 18,000 miles an hour and those space travelers tell us that day and night and the next day happen every 90 minutes. We scratch our heads in awe and wonder, asking what is time, and space, and life? Defining our worth and significance in such a universe seems almost impossible, if at all.

We live a spiritual life because our very nature cries out to reside amid the mystery that surrounds our existence. In spite of our seeming insignificance in this vast amount of space, we seek to become one with the vastness, to fill our hearts and minds with a sense of connection to it all. We are of the very stuff of that first big bang that shapes us, and we are drawn back to the very fundamental nature of things. We can call it scientific discovery that drives us, but even science presents us with more questions than answers. Therefore, I say what remains is spiritual; at the very center of things, there is awe and wonder. I call that a spiritual place.

In the everyday of our lives we read, meet, flush, talk, sing, aerobicize, fight, dance, mow the grass, find partners, eat lunch, make love, think, play, ask questions, marry, bury, are puzzled, get up early, divorce. We write, take risks, get up late, paint, jog, beg, cajole, buy, send, and save, and we don't often reflect on the awe and wonder of the space between electrons and neurons, or Mars and Jupiter, or the blue eyes of a one-minute-old newborn. But is it no wonder that at times in the midst of living, we want to pause, to stop, to catch our breath and in some form or other open ourselves "to whom it may concern"; to express our gratitude, our pain, our helplessness, our joy in the midst of what is beyond our complete knowing?

Is that not it? When we honestly stand before whatever life brings and contemplate our place amid the mystery, our finest response is to acknowledge our place in the vastness of time and space and the mundane and the majesty of the everyday. We cannot name that inner voice, that God beyond God, that light, that love that calls us or we call up, but in a moment when we say of ourselves to ourselves, "I am a wonder; I am a human being with eyes that see a match strike a mile away, who feels the pain of a tiny pinprick, who can love the unlovable, who makes more life and who finds the way of quarks and space stations. I, who am all this, I am even more than I can possibly understand." In those moments do we not pray the prayer of that singer of songs so many hundreds of years ago? *O God, what am I that you are mindful of me?* Is this not our universal prayer of awe and wonder and thanksgiving?

> Alla Renee Bozarth offers this prayer about prayer:
> ...be awake to the Life
> that is loving you and
> sing your prayer, laugh your prayer,
> dance your prayer, run
> and weep and sweat your prayer,
> sleep your prayer, eat your prayer,
> paint, sculpt, hammer and read your prayer,
> sweep, dig, rake, drive and hoe your prayer,
> garden and farm and build and clean your prayer,
> wash, iron, vacuum, sew, embroider and pickle your prayer,
> compute, touch, bend and fold but never delete
> or mutilate your prayer.
> Learn and play your prayer,
> work and rest your prayer,

fast and feast your prayer,
argue, talk, whisper, listen and shout your prayer,
groan and moan and spit and sneeze your prayer,
swim and hunt and cook your prayer,
digest and become your prayer,
release and recover your prayer,
breathe your prayer
be your prayer.[22]

Maybe our prayers are our deep conversations with life—what makes, sustains, and grows our life. In our deepest longings, in our darkest hours, and in our most joyful moments, our yearnings, our hopes, our inward and outward journeys of words and silence are our prayers. It is enough to allow them to be. Whatever is holy, divine, and of ultimate worth in the universe will guide us in those prayerful times.

When I walk out to my mailbox to get the morning paper, the grass is covered with dew, the purple irises stand tall under the crabapple tree and the evergreens beside the road stand stately. I am in awe. I sometimes say, "Thank you, purple iris; thank you, lily-of-the-valley; thank you, shaggy spruce; thank you, sparkling green fescue." I say it to no one in particular, but there is something in me that wants to give thanks for the beauty, the miracle, the wonder of all that is growing out of the dirt and all that is sustaining me.

When I am in deep despair and can utter only a cry for help, a searching appeal for guidance, I offer my prayer to whom it may concern, to something I know not what, perhaps to the divine mystery that surrounds and is within me.

In Barbara Kingsolver's *The Prodigal Summer*, it is Deanna who understood it when she looked at a dying luna moth in her hand. "A mystery caught in the hand," she said, "could lose its grace." So it is with prayer. It is a mystery that is part of the larger mystery and once completely caught loses itself.

The universe is an unfinished creation, and prayer is our communication with ourselves and all that is. Prayer may be one path to discovery and translation of how we are to be amid the mystery of which we are a part.

Questions for further reflection

1. Do you agree that prayers are our conversations with life? If not, what is prayer for you?
2. Is there something other than science that tells us about life? What does it mean to have a spiritual dimension to one's life?

Another Thanksgiving

When Columbus and his sailors came ashore in the Bahaman Islands, native Sarawak women and men greeted them and brought them food, water, and gifts. They were much like the Indians on the mainland, remarkable for their hospitality and their belief in sharing.

In his log, Columbus later wrote: "They brought us parrots and balls of cotton and spears and may other things, which they exchanged for the glass beads and hawks' bells. They willingly traded everything they owned. ...They do not bear arms, and do not know them, for I showed them a sword, they took it by the edge and cut themselves out of ignorance. ...Their spears are made of cane...they would make fine servants. ... With fifty men we could subjugate them all and make them do whatever we want."

On his second voyage to these lands, Columbus did not find any of the gold he had promised to bring back to his Spanish sponsors. Instead, he took 1,500 Sarawak men, women, and children captive. Of the 500 he forced to sail back to Spain, 200 died en route. Those who survived were sold as slaves. Columbus later wrote: "Let us in the name of the Holy Trinity go on sending all the slaves that can be sold."[23]

When he realized that there was no gold to be found that could be returned to Spain to repay his sponsors, Columbus had the native Indians rounded up to work as slaves on huge estates. Within two years, half the Indians on Haiti were dead, some by suicide to save themselves and their children from torture. Others were hanged or burned alive. By 1550, Columbus and his Spanish conquerors reduced the native population from 250,000 to 500.

The journal of a young priest, Bartolomé de las Casas, tells of these early conquests and provides much of the information regarding the Spaniards' behavior in their new world: "Two of these so-called Christians met two Indian boys one day each carrying a parrot; they took the parrots and for fun beheaded the boys."

In reviewing and writing early history, the treatment of heroes and their victims has been rewritten in favor of the victors. The distinguished historian, Samuel Eliot Morison of Harvard, notes: "[Columbus] had his faults, and his defects, but they were largely the defects of the qualities that made him great—his indomitable will, his superb faith in God and in his own mission as the Christ-bearer to lands beyond the seas, his stubborn persistence despite neglect, poverty and discouragement. But there was no flaw, no dark side to the most outstanding and essential of all his qualities—his seamanship."[24]

Morison's history includes Columbus' involvement in mass murder and calls it what it was: genocide. What he does in addition is to bury this fact in such a way that it becomes unimportant and hardly worth including as part of the readers' final estimate of the famous explorer's worth. Professor Howard Zinn notes: "To emphasize the heroism of Columbus and his successors as navigators and discoverers, and to de-emphasize their genocide, is not a technical necessity but an ideological choice. It serves—unwittingly—to justify what was done." What Columbus did to the Sarawak, Cortez did to the Aztecs, Pizarro to the Incas, and the English settlers of Virginia and Massachusetts to the Powhatans and the Pequots.

These and others have evidenced the human tendency to depersonalize those who are "other"—not white English, or not Puritans, or not European.

Before there was any permanent English settlement in Virginia, Richard Grenville landed there with seven ships. The

Indians he met were hospitable, but when one of them stole a small silver cup, Grenville sacked and burned the whole Indian village.

Fifty years after the Spanish inflicted their cruelties, the Pilgrims left England to settle in what was to become colonial America. The cruel New England winter had already set in when they landed. The Pilgrims were handicapped by their contract with the London merchant adventurers who had supplied the money for their voyage. No settler could work for his own gain. All they produced had to be placed in a common store. From it the people were given food and other necessities. When they traded with the Indians or cut and sawed timber, they had to ship the furs and lumber to London. The merchants were slow in forwarding supplies. Sometimes they sent over settlers who brought no provisions and had to be fed from the inadequately supplied stores.

The Pilgrims went through many hungry seasons. Their store of food was low and they were not skilled at hunting and fishing, nor were they equipped with fishing boats and gear. They developed scurvy or pneumonia. At times there were no more than six or seven healthy persons to care for the rest. Of the band of more than 100 Pilgrims who landed, half were dead before their first winter's end.

Soon after the Pilgrims arrived in Massachusetts, Squanto, a Pawtuxet native, befriended them, taught them how to survive in their new wilderness home, showed them how to plant crops, and acted as an interpreter with the neighboring Wampanoag tribe. The 1621 harvest was bountiful, and Squanto was probably present at the Pilgrims' first Thanksgiving celebration.

Nine years later, Squanto, along with other Indians, was seized by an English ship captain and sold into slavery in Spain. He escaped and eventually was taken back to New England. There he learned that his tribe had died from an epidemic, probably of smallpox brought by the English colonists. He settled in Plymouth and with another Indian taught the settlers to plant corn and to trap herring for fertilizer.

When the English were going through their first winter and many were literally starving to death, some of them ran off to live with the Powhatan Indians who fed and cared for them. When they did not return in the spring, the colonial governor sent a regiment of solders to seek revenge. They killed at least fifteen Indians, burned houses, and cut down the corn crop. He had the children of the queen drowned and the queen stabbed to death. Twelve years later, the Indians took their own revenge and massacred 347 men, women, and children. From then on, it was total war.

About this time, the governor of the Massachusetts Bay Colony, John Winthrop, created the excuse to take Indian land by declaring the area legally a "vacuum." The Indians, he said, "had not 'subdued' the land and therefore had only a 'natural' right to it, but not a 'civil right.' A 'natural right' did not have legal standing."

The Puritan followers of Winthrop took the biblical Psalms as their guide, particularly where it says, "Ask of me, and I shall give thee the heathen of thine inheritance and the uttermost parts of the earth for thy possession." To justify their use of force to take the land, they cited the Christian scriptures. In Paul's Letter to the Romans it says: "Whosoever therefore resisteth the power, resisteth the ordinance of God: and they that resist shall receive to themselves damnation."

The beloved preacher Dr. Cotton Mather wrote after one of the massacres at a Pequot village: "It was supposed that no less than 600 Pequot souls were brought to hell that day."

The number of Pequots in Connecticut was reduced to 21.

When NASA was preparing for the Apollo project, they did some astronaut training on a Navajo Indian reservation.

One day, a Navajo elder and his son were herding sheep and came across the space crew. The old man, who spoke only Navajo, asked a question, which his son translated. "What are the guys in the big suits doing?" A member of the crew said they were practicing for their trip to the moon. The old man got excited and asked if he could send a message to the moon with the astronauts.

Recognizing a promotional opportunity for the spin-doctors, the NASA folks found a tape recorder. After the old man recorded his message, they asked the son to translate. He refused. So the NASA reps brought the tape to the reservation, where the rest of the tribe listened and laughed, but refused to translate the elder's message. Finally, NASA called in an official government translator. He reported that the moon message said, "Watch out for these guys—they've come to steal your land."

Native American settlers had come some 25,000 years ago from Asia, across the land bridge of the Bering Straits to Alaska. They moved southward to North America, then to Central and South America. They numbered in total approximately 75 million, perhaps 25 million in North America when Columbus arrived. They developed hundreds of different tribal cultures and perhaps two thousand different languages. They perfected the art of agriculture and learned how to grow corn, which cannot grow by itself but must be planted, cultivated, fertilized, harvested, husked, and shelled. They also developed a variety of vegetables and fruits, as well as peanuts, chocolate, tobacco, and rubber.

Among these were the Zuñi and Hopi Indians, who were building villages consisting of large terraced multi-room buildings in the cliffs and mountains, a way of protecting themselves from their enemies. They created irrigation canals and dams, fired ceramics, wove baskets, and made cloth out of cotton, long before European settlers arrived to vanquish them.

In the Ohio River Valley, the Moundbuilders constructed thousands of enormous sculptures out of earth, sometimes in the shape of huge humans, birds, and serpents. They seem to have been part of a complex trading system of ornaments and weapons from as far off as the Great Lakes, the Far West, and the Gulf of Mexico.

The Iroquois nation, perhaps the largest of the Indian peoples in North America, was a complex, cooperative society, where land was owned and worked in common. Hunting was done together and the catch shared equally among members of the village. Women tended the crops and took charge of village affairs. They had no written language, but had their own laws, poetry, and an oral history and vocabulary, which included song, dance, and ceremonial drama more complex than any found in Europe at the same time.

It is clear that what most students of U.S. history have been taught has been twisted to reflect an European bias with the clear intention of ignoring native people's cultural and historical contributions, as though they were non-existent. Professor Zinn reminds us: "Columbus and his successors were not coming into an empty wilderness, but into a world which in some places were as densely populated as Europe itself, where the culture was complex, where human relations were more egalitarian than in Europe, and where the relations among men, women, children, and nature were more beautifully worked out than perhaps any place in the world."[25]

As more Europeans arrived in the United States and the white population increased, government opposition to these tribes grew stronger. In 1830, President Andrew Jackson announced: "The waves of population and civilization are rolling to the westward, and we now propose to acquire the countries occupied by the red men of the South and West by a fair exchange."

The next year, with support from Congress, Jackson demanded that all Indians inhabiting parts of Georgia and Alabama should emigrate beyond the Mississippi. Thirteen thousand Choctaws began a journey to a land and climate completely different from the one they knew. The first winter migration was one of the coldest on record, and hundreds died of pneumonia. Countless more died when summer heat brought a cholera epidemic.

There are more accounts of many other trails of tears. At Thanksgiving, and throughout the year, we ought to remind ourselves of another part of United States' heritage. Ours is a country blessed with abundant resources as well as caring and compassionate leaders. It also has a history of oppression, violence, and intolerance. The Irish and many other ethnic and religious groups have faced much of the same cruelty and discrimination they later applied to other minorities. The tendency continues today.

Therefore I conclude with this petition:

We pause before the mystery, the unknown of the next day or week or year. We pause before the incomprehensible that is around us. We give thanks amidst the unknown, for the riddles we unravel that lead us to new places, new ways of thinking and living.

We pause before the knowledge that we have been a part of the undoing of human dignity by accepting what is, rather than what is true.

We give thanks for a life that leads us to find answers to our questions of what to believe or whom to believe or where to follow.

We have not come this far alone. We pause to examine our life and the paths we have chosen, thankful for those who have nurtured us, guided us, supported us, and offered helping hands when we reached out in need.

Thankful we are for the laborers who sustain us, for those who patrol our streets, and fight our wars, and serve tirelessly in fire truck, garbage truck, ambulance, and bus. For those whose healing hands renew our bodies and minds. For those who produce the bounty from which our lives are maintained. To these and all who serve us in many unseen ways, we lift our thankful hearts.

For an earth of air and water from which life comes amid a vast universe beyond our imagining, we offer our hymn of praise and thanksgiving.

Questions for further reflection

1. What is the truth behind the discovery of America?
2. Beyond the traditional things for which we give thanks, what would you include in your Thanksgiving prayer?

Pain Got Us Here

One Tuesday morning, I bent over to get the dirty clothes out of my laundry basket. When I tried to straighten up, I felt a hot burn pass through the middle of my lower back. I groaned. I couldn't stand straight. In a few days, I was able to walk (a bit bent over), yet pain was the focus of my life. I was able to do a few other things I needed to do—load the clothes into the washing machine, do some grocery shopping, look over my email. But the pain was always there shaping whatever I did.

When we are in pain it takes over our life, or at least it becomes a major factor in it. Whatever else we are doing is secondary. No one needs to tell someone who has had kidney stones or a broken bone that pain can be all-consuming.

Our sensitivity to pain, however, goes beyond the sensation of bodily injury and discomfort. In addition to the physical world of pain, we live in a parallel world of thoughts and emotions that produces its own dangers and inflicts its own wounds. Psychic pain is as great if not greater than any pain caused by physical injury. It is the mingling of these two realms, the physical and the mental, that causes suffering. There is certainly a connection between pain and the soul.

Many creatures know pain; we humans know what it is to suffer. When a dog breaks a leg, it feels physical pain. When a man breaks a leg, he knows physical pain, but he also knows he might need an operation, that he may face a life in a wheelchair, he may never play soccer or run with his kids again. He may lose his job if he cannot perform as he once did or if his injury takes him away too long.

Pulitzer Prize-winning journalist Rick Bragg grew up dirt poor with a no-account father and a mother from whom goodness flowed in abundance. He writes, "We went to school at Spring Garden. In the first grade I fell in love with a little girl named Janice, Janice Something. But the first grade was divided into a rigid caste system by the ancient teacher, and I was placed clear across the room from her. They named the sections of the divided classroom after birds. She was a Cardinal, one of the children of the well-to-do who studied from nice books with bright pictures, and I was a Jaybird, one of the poor or just plain dumb children who got what was left after the good books were passed out. Our lessons were simplistic, and I could always read. I memorized the simple reader, and the teacher was so impressed she let me read with the Cardinals one day. I did not miss a word, but the next day I was back with the Jaybirds. The teacher—and I will always, always remember this—told me I would be much more comfortable with my own kind. I was six, but even at six you understand what it means to be told you are not good enough to sit with the well-scrubbed."[26]

There is physical pain, and there is psychological pain.

Anthropologists tell us that it was pain that got us where we are in human evolution. Simple animals and plants with life spans numbering only a few weeks or months come equipped with all the knowledge they need to survive; pain's lessons would be wasted on them. Pain is our teacher, the guide in nature's school of survival. An ant runs ahead of a fire because instinct tells it to, but it is not something it learned from experience. Pain only matters to organisms with an advanced talent for learning, remembering, and adapting. So, for us, pain is not synonymous with life; it is synonymous with intelligence.

Unless we humans decide to eradicate them, and at the rate we are going we just might, most plants and animals survive because there are plenty of them to go around. A deer eats the leaves off a tree, but the tree survives because the tree produces more leaves than it needs to carry on, so it can share with the deer and survive.

However, for some life forms there was a need to survive based not on abundance or mass production, but on the continuation of the individual creature. In their peak reproductive period, women can produce just a single infant each year, and a decade or longer will pass before that infant achieves any semblance of independence. We are a fragile bunch. Compared to other species, our hearing is poor, our eyesight even worse. We are slow of foot and if we don't eat for a day we are ravenous. We feel comfortable only in a narrow temperature range. Humanity's upright posture frees our hands for useful things, but it also makes us easily seen and prone to falling down—or hurting our backs bending over for the laundry. We have been building homes, donning clothes, eating meat, and manipulating our surroundings since we emerged from the cave. We control our environment not because we can but because we must out of biological necessity. Pain, or at least our desire to avoid pain, has moved us to find alternative ways of surviving.

This pain we have lived with since forever continues to mystify us. The writer C.S. Lewis has suggested that God allows suffering to command our attention. Pain, for Mr. Lewis, is the Divine Megaphone through which God speaks. Without pain we would not heed our maker nor pay him honor. Lewis is suggesting that God had the power to create a world free of pain, but chose not to do so out of fear of being rendered unneeded, ignored, and irrelevant. That may be, but I suspect something else is going on.

While Rick Bragg was writing and reporting for *The New York Times*, a tornado ripped through the town near where he grew up. The winds destroyed a country church, killing fourteen adults and six children. When the storm hit, the children were putting on a play. There were screams of pain and fear. Most of those who were killed died instantly.

Bragg traveled home to write the second day story about this tragedy. "This is a place," he wrote, "where grandmothers hold babies in their laps under the stars and whisper in their ears that the lights in the sky are holes in the floor of heaven. This is a place where the song, 'Jesus Loves Me' has rocked generations to sleep, and heaven is not a concept, but a destination. Yet in this place where many things, even storms, are viewed as God's will, people strong in their faith and their children have died in, of all places, a church. The destruction of this little country church and the deaths—included the pastor's vivacious four-year-old daughter—have shaken the faith of many people in the deeply religious corner of Alabama, about eighty miles northeast of Birmingham. It is not that it has turned them against God, only that it has hurt them in a place usually safe from a hurt, like a bruise on the soul."[27]

Bragg reminds us that few if any are spared pain. When he suggested that God allows suffering to call us to attention, C.S. Lewis missed the point. Suffering is not a megaphone nor is it a rod of punishment; rather, it is an inevitable consequence of being alive and aware. To be conscious is to suffer; it is part of how we got here. There is no answer to why pain exists, yet because it is our teacher it helps to speak of it, to tell of how it feels, and what it may mean for us.

Sickle cell anemia is a blood disease common in African-Americans. In the sickle cell disease, the normally round red blood cells become deformed into nonfunctioning sickle-shaped cells, hence the name. Some who get a single copy of the gene have a mild deformity of their blood cells. Those who carry two copies, one from each parent, often die in childhood or early adolescence.

Yet we are learning from studies of native African populations that people with the sickle cell trait seem to be immune from malaria. This means that the mild predisposition to sickle cell anemia saves more lives from malaria than will be lost through the full-blown sickle cell disease.

Full blown cystic fibrosis is lethal, but those with a mild genetic predisposition to CF may be protected against typhoid and cholera. Full-blown Tay-Sachs disease, a neurological disorder endemic to Jewish populations, is also lethal, but researchers are saying a mild genetic predisposition may protect against tuberculosis.[28]

I share these medical findings to remind us that what may appear as injurious may contain a life-saving gift. I do not wish to minimize or trivialize pain. It can be, and sometimes is, debilitating, all-consuming, and life destroying. Living with pain often means great suffering; those experiencing it deserve care and concern. It would be simplistic and inappropriate to suggest that all pain has a purpose. Yet if the anthropologists and our experiences are right, pain may also contain a gift.

I certainly don't know what my back pain was good for, but perhaps it was to remind me that I am human, that I am fragile, that I ought to take better care of myself, that I ought to slow down, be a bit more mindful of what is central to my being, to take better care of my soul.

The Rev. Dr. Powell Davies once said that life was just a chance to grow a soul. I would add that pain is part of growing that soul, for it is part of being alive. We cannot live without experiencing pain, and we cannot grieve or suffer if we have not loved or cared deeply about something or someone.

We all know pain—our lives are not complete without it—so perhaps it is not pain we ought to fear, but lives without pain; empty lives, lives that do not know love or challenge or lives that do not build on the gifts we have been given. In these things we may discover pain; we may also uncover our soul.[29]

Perhaps knowing that pain is what we share, that it is what got us here, serves to remind us of what we ought to treasure: the good in our lives, the good we have done to bring us here, what love has given us, and what our reaching out can offer to another. We risk pain when we work, when we play, when we offer our hand to another, when we commit to be in that place for which it is good to have stood. To risk pain is a way of creating our soul.

A friend told me over lunch about some of the famous people he knew—several renowned authors and political figures, names we all have heard of. As he was talking, what came to my mind was that the experiences of these rich, powerful, and famous people were no more exemplary than many people I know who are relatively unknown but whose lives are as noble and brave and charismatic as the notables of whom my friend was speaking. What made each of them exemplary was the suffering they had faced in their lives.

Many who would be called ordinary folk have struggled with issues that have required strength and courage; many have lived through pain, both physical and psychological, demonstrating a depth of character that is admirable and from which others can learn and grow.

Philosopher Elizabeth Spelman suggests that one of the values of suffering is that it acts as a bank. Suffering is the human condition in which the experiences of some can be put to good use by others. Whatever benefits may be extracted from particular forms of suffering need not belong only to those who have endured them, but give witness to that from which others can draw.[30]

I know many of you reading this have contributed to the bank that offers strength and wisdom and comfort to others, because you have been willing to live and to suffer nobly. Your pain has been part of the bank out of which you contribute to the world.

I suspect that to ourselves we're pretty ordinary, at least on most days, but some days we surprise ourselves. Some days we're not ordinary at all, as when we teach a right principle that someone lives by forever, or when we take the dish of stew to someone in a jam, or laugh out loud about our own mistakes, or when we manage to confront what we must in looking toward what is ahead, or when we cry with a neighbor in her grief. Pain taught us these things.

Pain has brought us here, from millions of years to now and from the lives of those who made our lives possible. The humiliation and pain Rick Bragg experienced as a Jaybird in that backwater school may have had more to do with his winning a Pulitzer than anything he might have learned at a prestigious school of journalism. It is what we've learned from our pain that makes us more than ordinary. Pain is our teacher. Let us listen to what it has to tell us.

Questions for further reflection

1. What psychological pain have you suffered, and how did you deal with it?
2. Have you suffered from pain other than psychological? If so, how was it different from psychological pain?
3. Can you think of ways suffering has benefited you? Or have you used it to help others?

A Free Path, Or What

What religious terrorists have in common is a view of the world as a site of cosmic struggle in which the forces of evil threaten the forces of good. Their theology evolves in a context of injury or threat. Holy warriors experience themselves as victims of an enemy's unjustified aggression and violence. Having been humiliated, they are fighting back to restore honor for their people and to pay back injustices. They believe their own deaths will bring glory to their families, will be honored among the people, and will be pleasing to God. Acts of religious terrorism may not defeat the enemy; the acts may not even have a military or political objective. Theologian Mark Juergensmeyer studies those whose beliefs lead them to become religious terrorists. He says that the meaning of the acts is religious—an act of faithful defiance of evil to declare one's devotion to God. Theirs is a theology that says God saves through violence.

This is not a new notion. It is shared by many of the world's major religions and has been a core doctrine of Western Christianity for the past thousand years. The first Crusade, under Pope Urban II, called in 1095, urged holy warriors to sacrifice their lives just as Jesus gave his on the cross. The Pope promised that their noble deaths would merit the forgiveness of debts and garner rewards to the slain soldiers' families. These promises were based on the formulations of an eleventh-century theologian, Anselm of Canterbury, who suggested that Jesus died on the cross to pay for the injury to God's honor caused by human sin. His writings were written to defend Christianity from Muslims and Jews. The Pope's decrees led to the slaughter of thousands of innocent people.

This sounds so much like those who sought revenge by flying airplanes into the World Trade Center and who blow up buses, hospitals, and schools in the name of Jewish or Muslim rights. They say God is on their side, a God who sanctions the destruction of their enemies and who executes justice through retaliation.[31]

The Middle East is filled with war. It reminds me of how far we have not come from the cave we first lived in as human beings. I fear that what drives us is the notion that might makes right. I wonder how far we have to go before love rather than hate motivates much of humanity.

Starhawk, the award-winning author on eco-justice, at times calls herself a mystic, sometimes a witch; other times, a teacher, an author, a Jew. A few years ago, she visited a refugee camp in Palestine where Israeli forces had rounded up 4,000 men, leaving the camp to women and children. The men offered no resistance, no battle.

As she tells it, at night, gunfire and explosions fill the air. With two companions, Starhawk is taken to a home in the camp. "Welcome, welcome," says Samar, as she offers refuge in the three small rooms that house her family, which includes her mother, nieces and nephews, and her brother's wife Hanin, who is six months pregnant. Tea is served amid sounds of the Israelis blowing up houses nearby. "Yahoud!" the women cry after the sound of the explosion subsides. Yahoud is the Arabic word for Jew. They talk of the baby to come, a boy they believe. Starhawk, a Yahoud, is welcomed and shares a bed with Hanin and two children.

The next day Israeli troops arrive at the house. Starhawk and her companions go out to talk with them. The soldiers know two of those in the house, Jessica and Melissa. Ahmed, a young boy, is terrified, yet runs toward the soldiers crying. "Take off your helmet," Jessica asks the soldiers. "Help him be not so afraid."

A soldier takes off his helmet, and Ahmed's cries subside. Samar holds the little boy up to the soldier's face, tells him to give the soldier a kiss. She doesn't want Ahmed to be afraid, to hate. The little boy kisses the soldier. The soldier kisses him back and hands him a small Palestinian flag.

Then the soldiers search the house, pulling everything off the walls, out of the closets, and dumping everything in piles on the floor. The wood paneling is punched full of holes, couches overturned, bags of grain emptied into the sink. Broken glass litters the floor. When the soldiers leave the family begins to clean up while Hanin cooks supper. "For us this is normal," she says.

The third night the soldiers return and this time no kisses. They lock everyone in a room and begin a rampage through the house, ripping paneling off the walls, knocking holes in the tile floor and the concrete beneath. They smash and destroy, then urinate on the mess they have left. The house has been turned into a wrecking yard, and nothing has been found. When Hanin, the pregnant mother, emerges and sees what has happened she goes into shock. She is resilient and strong, but this assault has gone beyond "normal." She breaks down. Those around her fear she may lose the baby, and they finally convince a soldier who is also a paramedic to take her to the hospital. The baby and Hanin survive, but she is broken, her eyes have lost their light. "Hanin loves you," she writes on a note to Starhawk, the Yahoud, the Jew.

What are we to make of a world that offers kindness to strangers, while others bring suffering? What are we to make of a world that raises fundamental questions about right and wrong, truth and justice, and largely transforms religious truth into bitter hatred and warfare?

Israel claims to be a state governed by the Torah, Palestine by the Koran, and some believe the United States should be run by the Christian scriptures. Ours is a world where religion, at its best, is modeled on love, compassion, and generosity, but in reality it is often used as a fearful defense against the modern world. Some forms of fundamentalist Christianity, Judaism, and Islam see spiritual bankruptcy everywhere, tainted by scientific discovery and technology, and use violence to have their way.

There is, in the minds of these who would inflict their truth on the rest of us, the notion that there is peace through pain. It is a plan adopted by countless United States administrations, as well as leaders in the West Bank, Jerusalem, Baghdad, Pyongyang, and Tehran.

In the midst of this turning of religion's fundamental truth of compassion and love on its head, the Rev. Dr. Rebecca Parker, reminds us, "Love embraces the goodness of this world and seeks paradise on earth, a heaven of mutual respect. Love generates life—from the first moment of conception of a child, to the last moment when love creates a way for those who have died to be remembered with gratitude and tenderness. And in the deepest night, when our hearts are breaking, it is the discovery of a love that chooses unshakeable fidelity to our common humanity that renews us and redirects us to a life of generosity."[32]

I hear these words, and at times I respond with, "How sentimental, how naïve, how trite and overworked." Speaking of love in this way will not suffice if we are merely idealistic. Dr. Parker adds however, "Love is more than idealism. It is wisdom."

A love that is more than sentiment is love that you and I bring forth and make present in the midst of the daily grind. This love is embedded in the nitty-gritty of life. Love gives more than lip service to our religion, whatever form it takes. Love is what gives religion a voice, a presence in the world.

Many argue that a religion based on love is outmoded, irrelevant for today's world. The way to truth and human understanding is scientific reason and psychological discovery. Science explains how this universe, of which we are only a very tiny speck, works. This suggests that the Darwinian view of life excludes any notion of a first mover or creator. James Watson, the co-discoverer of the molecular structure of the DNA molecule, declares that "one of the greatest gifts science has brought to the world is continuing elimination of the supernatural." Yet at the same time there is a growing debate in the courts, classrooms, and houses of religion regarding the intelligent design of the universe, with some very thoughtful people arguing that there is a creator or creative force that established all this wonder.

I remain in the dark about the ultimate truth of the claims of science and religion, but have a sense that these different ways of understanding are connected. Science is about the natural material world and religion about the spiritual world. As one letter to the editor in the *New York Times* puts it, "There is no contradiction between evolution and religion. One explains how, and the other explains why."

The Nobel Prize winner, physicist Richard Feynman, writes about flowers and says, "I have a friend who's an artist. ...He'll hold up a flower and say, 'Look how beautiful this is, but you as a scientist, oh, take this all apart and it becomes a dull thing.' And I think that he's kind of nutty. ...I can appreciate the aesthetic beauty of a flower. At the same time, I see much more about the flower than he sees. I can imagine the cells in there, the complicated actions inside that also have a beauty. I mean, it's not just beauty at this dimension of one centimeter, there is also beauty at a smaller dimension, the inner structure. ...All kinds of interesting observations show that science knowledge only adds to the excitement and mystery and the awe of a flower. It only adds; I do not understand how it subtracts." [33]

As Dr. Feynman reminds us, science teaches us about the flowers by adding to the mystery. Science enhances our sense of wonder and awe that is in the opening petals and the stamens within. As our scientific understanding of the flower grows, so can our appreciation of its beauty and its incredible complexity. An enlightened religion grows out of that kind of knowing, which makes our world more understandable. What it reveals increases its grandeur, its mystery, and its glorious splendor and acknowledges our connection to all things. It is the connection between heart and mind, mystery and reason that is the tension with which we live and gives truth to our life. Neither a scientific or religious world view alone is sufficient for life. A healthy regard for both is not only helpful but necessary.

The discussion of scientific and religious truth is vitally important given the conditions under which human beings seem to be living these days. The world is in trouble; it is at war, millions die from diseases that could be cured, hunger stalks countless children from birth to their early deaths. Suffering often occurs in a world where science is excluded and only a religious world view is tolerated. An enlightened religion that includes serious scientific reason only adds, it does not subtract, from that world. An enlightened religion encompasses our passions, our experience, and our intellect. It is the connection between heart and mind that we must keep before us.

Dr. Parker reminds us, "We are to proclaim what is moral, what is just, what reverences life, what gives hope in the face of violence, what restores life when it has been fractured by human cruelty, what is worthy of our ultimate loyalty, what sustains us in the long night of pain, what connects us in the right relationship to our neighbor, what saves the world." That is the way of an enlightened religion.

As I hear myself relay these words, I recall that I have said words like them before. They are similar to words you have heard many times. Yet, I need to be informed by them again for they are fundamental to my understanding of religion. Religion is not about finding the right theological truth or the ultimate creed by which to live. Religion is about living with love as our guide.

In a world where soldiers destroy homes and lives at will, where religions vie for the most violent path to peace, and where women and children suffer from malnutrition and disease for no reason other than they live under uncaring leaders, we are called in our tiny corner of the universe to walk together in love. It is so trite to say, yet so fundamentally true. It means loving not only those who love back, but those who hate back or destroy the lovely, the beautiful, the true. Science will discover the facts of our existence, but it will not keep Jews from house-wrecking rampages upon Palestinians, nor will it keep Christians from warring against Muslims. Ironically, it is the loving form of those religions that is the guide to being whole.

Questions for further reflection

1. The United States is governed by the Constitution. Would it be helpful if the Bible were more or less influential in governing?
2. Do you believe that religion is about finding the right theological truth? Or do you believe that religion is about living with love as our guide? Or both?

It's the Process, Maybe

Scientists now believe that the human family goes back some six million years, when human creatures began to walk upright and diverged from chimpanzees and gorillas. Recently, a 3.5-million-year-old skull belonging to an entirely new branch of the human family was uncovered in Kenya by Meave Leakey, now the standard-bearer of the famous fossil-hunting family.[34]

From the cranium and partial jaw, Dr. Leakey and her colleagues determined that the individual was unlike its contemporary hominid known as Lucy, who was once the oldest found specimen and whose face resembled a chimpanzee. The Leakey specimen was flat faced with small teeth and seemed to resemble the look of later hominids. What Dr. Leakey concluded from her finding is that this creature is completely different from anything else in the hominid family. It is likely that there were several, if not many, species of humans living long before Lucy,

Paleontologists now say that evolution is not simply a generation-to-generation change in genes, but rather a process of complex factors including competition for food and adaptation to the environment, which have contributed to setting human beings on their particular journey.

For two billion years, give or take a few million, life stagnated amid a scum of single-celled bacteria and algae covering the earth. Then, for reasons still obscure, there was an explosion of multi-cellular life. In a matter of some ten million years, give or take a couple million, primitive precursors of nearly all the family of plants and animals now known emerged.

Turning to another recent discovery, scientists working in China uncovered fossils of a tiny half-a-billion-year-old creature christened *Yunnanozoon lividum*, which seems to have the vestigial traces of a spinal cord. Speculation has it that this creature is a distant uncle rather than great-grandfather of Homo sapiens. Some scientists hypothesize from this finding that the human blueprint, with its long spinal column bulging on one end with a mushy gray protuberance called a brain, may not be the outcome of a long process of evolutionary crafting. This form of life may not have evolved over millions of years, but was crawling about from the very beginning of this Cambrian period in history.

These speculations about evolutionary explosions, primal creatures, and the twists and turns of humanoid history are a way of understanding our ancestry and our spiritual path. To help us understand the interconnected nature of our lives, author and essayist Mary Oliver writes, "At our town's old burn dump, not officially used for years, discarded peppermint and raspberries reconnected their roots to the gravelly earth and went on growing; a couple of apple trees blossomed and bore each year a bushel of green and bumpy fruit. Blackberries drifted up and down the slopes; thistles, bouncing bet, everlasting, goldenrod, wild carrot lifted their leaves and then their flowers and then their rafts of seeds. Honeysuckle, in uplifted waves, washed toward some pink roses, no longer a neat and civilized hedge but a thorny ledge, with darkness at its hem."[35]

Mary Oliver's burn dump is no more. On these few acres of land Oliver describes, the city will build its latest sewage facility, an operation that has become a necessity given the greatly expanding population of this Cape Cod village.

From primal Lucy to Oliver's town dump there is a continuum, a journey that is an interconnected web of which all of us are a part, and you and I are left with questions about where we fit in this journey. Are we connected to anything or anyone larger than ourselves? According to philosopher and mathematician Alfred North Whitehead, "The universe is not a random assortment of lifeless particles, rather an ensemble of interrelated and dynamic goings-on that are seemingly miraculous by their very nature. We participate in those dynamics as we act out our lives. Creation's path changes because of the choices and decisions we make."

In the mid-1800s, the physiologist Michel Chevreul showed that a spot of pure color on the retina is always accompanied by its complement; the eye sees a dot of orange rimmed by a halo of blue. Red is ringed by green, purple by yellow. The interference of these visual haloes means that each color affects its neighbor. So it is with every organism. Relationships between parent and offspring, predator and prey, population and food supply—each enable it to live and in turn touch and transform the other. That is the process of life.

That process means we are connected, from that early primate to the raccoon scavenging in Mary Oliver's town dump. As we live out our lives making choices, we shape the future as well as the present. That process is part of the bigger picture, the larger whole of which our lives and our actions are a small but significant part. We are the meaning makers.

In the search for meaning we find the truth for our lives, not in fixed answers but in answers that satisfy for now but will change as discoveries tumble around us. Discoveries have emerged from reflecting on very ancient bones and trash dumps laden with spilt oils, paints, and car batteries, amid wild carrot, blackberries, and goldfinches, only to remind us that we are part of an ongoing creation, a process that we shape by the virtuous and the shameless acts we carry out.

As Whitehead explains, "Every entity is only to be understood in terms of the way in which it is interwoven with the rest of the universe."

Creation is in our hands. We shape the direction that life takes. We are the creators of good and evil, and if good is to prevail, we are the ones who will make it happen.

Questions for further reflection

1. Do you believe we are connected to anything or anyone larger than ourselves? If so, what?
2. If we are not connected to anything else, what are the guiding principles in your life?
3. How is "creation in our hands?" Or is it?

Concerning Our Living and Our Dying

Poet Nancy Wood writes:
You will ask
What good are dead leaves
And I will tell you
They nourish the sore earth.
You shall ask
What reason is there for winter
And I will tell you
To bring about new leaves.
You shall ask
Why are the leaves so green
And I will tell you
Because they are rich with life
You shall ask
Why must summer end
And I will tell you
So that the leaves can die.

I knew Andrew[36] quite well about the time he discovered, like his mother, that he had Alzheimer's disease, or something akin to it, for he could sense that his mind was not always tracking as it should, and his wife could still report to him about his forgetfulness.

I remember sitting with him on the back porch of his very modern home. We talked about how he had watched his mother's life deteriorate, and how he once found her wandering outside without any clothes. He was afraid. "Richard," he said to me, "I am not afraid to end my life, but I want to do it when the time is right. I don't want to do it while I still have the ability to make decisions and choose. Yet if I wait too long, and I turn the corner, then my mind will be too far gone, and I can't make the decision."

The Catch-22 situation, for most who have such a crippling mental disease, is that by the time you want to die you are unable to do anything about it. So it was for Andrew. He passed the time when he could decide for himself how he would die, be it suicide or a hospital order not to resuscitate or by an "accident of some kind." Eventually, he could not complete sentences and did not know where he was.

Many of you could tell similar stories. The question before us is what should we do? That is the question I will leave you with after you read the thoughts I offer now.

Janet Adkins had been a musician and a teacher. She regularly forgot the music she loved or what *Hamlet* was about and couldn't remember what the main themes were in *War and Peace*. (Come to think of it, neither can I.) She did not want to face the future with her mind forgetting more and more. She could have taken a gun or driven her car into a bridge abutment, but she wanted a gentle death. She talked with her minister and her friends and then with Jack Kavorkian, known to many as doctor death.

The writer and former *New York Times* columnist Anna Quindlen notes that there is a message in the Janet Adkins case. "It illustrates," writes Quindlen, "how desperate we have become to retain some modicum of control in the face not only of horrible illness, but of medical protocols that lengthen degeneration and dying." Death and dying are not easy topics to discuss, but the more we understand death the better we will understand life.

There are few of us who want to end our lives while we are still well and surrounded by friends and loved ones we still know and recognize, but after the chemotherapy and surgeries, and the lengthy progressions of our disease, some of us become less than ourselves. We are still alive, but without any semblance of the self we once were. What then?

One obvious question that Janet Adkins raises for all of us is whether individuals have the right to take their own lives, particularly in face of suffering and the loss of quality of life. We might ask ourselves if there is ever a time when people who see no future for themselves have the right to terminate their own lives. Do we have the permission, ultimately, to choose to die when we want to?

Some say yes, arguing that we have the obligation to control much of the rest of our lives so we should also have the right of this most basic form of control, whether we live or die.

Others argue that those who would take their lives, by the very fact that they want to die, are not in a competent state of mind to decide, for that decision goes against our deepest instinct to survive.

What has added complexity to this debate is the ability of the medical system to keep us alive in early and late stages of life as never before. Fetuses only twenty-six weeks old can now survive outside the womb. Now more of us can grow older than ever before due to modern medical miracles.

As a society we ask for the best in medical care. When we are ill we want all the technology possible at our disposal. We ask physicians to make us well again. In those moments we ask them to keep us alive. With this debate about end of life, however, we have put them in a reverse position. The same physicians we ask to keep us alive we now ask to put us to death. On the one hand we ask for all means necessary to sustain life, on the other we want to decide for ourselves whether we should live or die. While we want to decide about our living and our dying, we must also consider the dilemma that choice puts upon our families and loved ones as well as the healthcare providers we ask to treat us.

When we ask about life, then we must ask about the quality of life and about death as well. These are the spiritual issues we must raise as we think about healthcare reform. We know there must be limits to life itself. Health care is part of setting those limits.

Most people shaping the debate set forth by several of the candidates who recently ran for the office of President saw health care as an economic and political issue. In fact, it is a deeply religious issue, because first we should ask, "What is the meaning of our lives?" Currently this country's citizens are talking both emotionally and seriously about who will get what level of health care, who will define the nature of that care, what is the obligation we have to provide that care, and to what extent should care be given or withheld, as well as how should the costs for such care be met.

These are some of the questions raised by the current health care debate, but there are many other questions as well. Whether or not we trust our elected officials to raise the right questions, it would be difficult for even the highest-minded and courageous to find a way to create a medical system that will work for everyone. The task is incredibly complex with opposing values and ideals that no Solomon with all his wisdom can easily resolve.

We have to ask, who will define the limits to care? Who will decide who is to live and who is to die, or who will get a kidney transplant and who will not? If our country agrees to provide health care for all, then is there anything the society can require of the individual in return? Do lawmakers have the right to set limits on who will get care? Ought there be limits to the care that is offered? If you are a person who continually abuses alcohol or other drugs or if you lead a high-risk lifestyle can society place limits on the amount of care you will receive?

Let us assume for a moment that religion is our response to the fact of being born and the reality of our death. These questions of health care lead us to fundamental religious questions: What is the nature of human life? What is a human being's ultimate worth? Who decides if Janet Adkins's life ought to continue? Should she be the soul judge of that or should the state? Should someone who has a debilitating disease be considered competent to decide to end her life? The answers to those questions are inherent in the deliberations before us and may or may not be answered as we work out a national healthcare program.

While these issues are far more complex than we can possibly resolve there is no better place for the debate to occur than where people care about the quality of human life and the nature of life itself. That is why we must struggle with these issues and why we must have a voice in how to carry out health-care reform.

Therefore, I suggest we begin the debate with the notion that life should be determined in terms of meaning not in terms of longevity.

I share the concern of those like my friend who had Alzheimer's disease and others facing deteriorating health that they may lose the power to decide whether to continue their lives. I do not advocate that life be ended when health remains and the possibilities are present to offer love and gentleness and goodness to the world. Sadly, the one who wants to die is often led to believe such a decision is best made by our society, a consumer-driven culture that already puts too much value on productivity and monetary success. There are so many subtle messages we receive that say we don't have worth that I am afraid when we encourage the right to die we may be reflecting the stigmas attached to illness or job loss or poverty or physical handicap.

Do we not regularly experience subtle messages that we are of little worth? I regularly have to retrieve the weekly newspaper from the middle of my driveway or the bushes. The man who has promised to fix my furnace never shows, and after repeated calls, finally only fixes it half right. Lowe's will sell me most anything at a relatively low price, but regularly it breaks after only a few uses. How often it is when we're out for a drive that someone in a great hurry rides our rear bumper till we are forced to move over so he or she can fly by on their way to who knows where. I don't need to take these things personally. These are busy people with many things on their mind, and they don't intend to injure me with their thoughtlessness. However, by not caring or ignoring my feelings and my life, they send the message that I'm not worth the bother.

What if I am gay, or African-American, or physically handicapped, or female and regularly receive messages that I am of less worth than healthy, heterosexual white males? Would I not be in a position to value my life less and then be less willing to want to live? To then allow me to take my own life, society may only be reinforcing those negative messages of my worth. What if I am seriously ill and not fully industrious? Would I then be made to feel that I was of little worth and better off not using up dollars that might be spent for someone who is going to be productive?

Nowhere are these messages more evident than in old age. Often in our society the point is made that the elderly are of less worth than the young. Old age is the last phase of life. To live in this phase successfully requires recognition of decline and loss, that life is coming to an end and this is the time to make sense of oneself and one's place in relation to those who will come after. It is a time to allow the young to accept responsibility and leadership. I share, however, with the medical ethicist Daniel Callahan, the concern that those who are aging or ill will feel that the only way they can regain self-control over their lives is to have available the possibility of suicide.[37] In our youth-obsessed culture, ageism can creep in and devalue the worth of the elderly. Do we not risk subjecting the elderly to questions of their worth by even suggesting that it is possible for them to legally end their life? Do they hear in that a wish on our part that they are no longer of value when we allow medically assisted suicide as a ready option? Those questions must be balanced with the request of those who are suffering and asking for complete relief.

There is also the practical question of, who pays? We are in the midst of a debate that has sharply divided our country between those who argue that health care is a basic right against others who say individuals ought to be responsible for the costs of their care. But as Bishop John Shelby Spong notes, "When the choice is made that a society will provide basic quality health care to all its citizens, then that society must also set the limits beyond which that health care cannot go."

If we are to provide for the young as well as the old, we must ask about how much care we should provide. Is there a time when the medical profession must say "no" to a heart transplant when it will only extend life another year? Or "no" to a kidney transplant to someone over sixty-five? The issue is, in part, what do we mean by a normal life span? How do we determine when a life is complete?

Let me suggest that a natural life span means one whose life opportunities have, to some degree at least, been fulfilled. I realize there is, for most of us, never completion of those things we would like to do, but the most interesting and creative lives will always have more to do and death will always cut short what is out there yet waiting to be done. It is a question of what has been done that matters. If one has lived long enough to fulfill a time of loving and useful work, a life with others, the pursuit of moral ideals, the experiences of beauty and travel, then perhaps he or she has lived a natural life span, no matter how old.

Conceivably the time of dying should be after one has accomplished the possibilities life holds, after the moral obligations to those for whom one has responsibility are completed, and when one's death will not seem to others an offense to sense or sensibility. It may seem harsh to suggest that modern medicine should not be mandated in every case to prolong life, but such a mandate compels us to come to terms with our finitude and is part of what helps us give meaning to our life.

Medicine should be used to help us realize our natural and fitting life span and thereafter for the relief of suffering. That means not just more life as such, but life free of whatever pain and suffering might impede our goals of a rewarding existence.

Even if there were unlimited resources to sustain life forever there are ample reasons why a life that is without meaning should not be prolonged. There can come a time when no more should be done to sustain life.

It was Janet Adkins's decision that her life no longer was full. For her, life was no longer as she wished it to be; it was without joy or purpose or hope. She chose to die a gentle death. For us, who remain behind, we ask whether she had the right to choose to die. What is our part in leading her to that choice, and how will we decide if such be a choice we must make?

Questions for further reflection

1. Would you be able to assist someone who wanted help with his/her suicide?
2. Should there be an age past which no special means to keep a dying or terminally ill patient alive should be allowed?
3. What guidelines should be applied regulating the use of organs to assist those in need of them?

The Courage to Be

I want to remind you that it takes courage just to be, and in particular, the religious journey requires a valiant heart.

I began thinking about this a while ago when I came across an article by a colleague of mine. Several things he said about the yes's and no's of life meant a lot to me.

In my life, as I suspect it is for many of you, I hear many affirmations along with many negatives. I hear yes's and no's, but the no's seem so much louder than the yes's. I want to remind you that it takes courage to live amid the no's.

The screen-testing director at MGM Studios wrote for his files, "Fred Astaire—can't act, slightly balding, can dance a little." Louisa May Alcott, before she wrote *Little Women*, was encouraged by her family to work as a servant or seamstress.

One of Enrico Caruso's early teachers said he had no voice at all and could not sing, and Beethoven's teacher said he was hopeless as a composer.

Rodin's uncle said his nephew was a dolt, F. W. Woolworth's first employer said he did not have enough sense to wait upon customers, Walt Disney was fired by a newspaper editor for his lack of ideas, and Richard Bach was turned down by eighteen publishers before someone decided to give *Jonathan Livingston Seagull* a try.[38]

Many of us have had someone, or several people, say to us, "Oh, you'll never amount to much," maybe not in so many words, but by an offhand comment that brought discouragement to an idea or plan we had in mind. The no's come in many ways, but they come in such a way that our first reaction is to give up on a dream.

There was the promise of a marriage that would last forever, but no longer provides what you hoped. You settle on a job instead of the dream of a promising career because responsibilities to family call you to take fewer risks. Age is creeping up, and the energy or drive is just not available as it once was. Illness has taken its toll on a partner, and plans for the future are set aside to make do for what must be taken care of now.

We only have, however, what is now, what we can do with what we have, and it may mean facing the wall, the barrier, the pit, the emptiness with a brave heart.

We need courage when we fail at life, or love, or work, or duty. We need courage when knowledge fails, when uncertainty grips us, when darkness surrounds us, when despair engulfs us and we cannot move.

In his book *Another Roadside Attraction*, Tom Robbins writes: "Real courage is risking something that might force you to rethink your thoughts and suffer change and stretch consciousness. Real courage is risking one's clichés."

It takes an amazing kind of courage to risk one's life for another. Most of us won't ever have to face that possibility, although I know that some of you have. I do know you have risked rethinking your thoughts, suffered change, and stretched your consciousness.

I want to give a few examples of how some I have known or know now have faced change and the yes's and no's.

I know of someone who is facing chemotherapy with a good sense of humor. Another assists a family member who is bedridden. Another each day goes to work while living with almost constant pain. You know of someone who has had to decide whether or not to turn off life-support equipment sustaining someone she loves. Several of you have said to a coworker, "I did not appreciate that homophobic joke." Some of you live with insistent no's in your head, saying you'll never be enough, yet you carry on with your yes.

In early 2011, we witnessed the courage of some fifty nuclear reactor engineers and maintenance men and women stand forth in the face of a lifetime of radiation sickness, taking on a huge no and saying yes by their willingness to risk their lives for others.

Howard Thurman writes: "Courage is not a blustering manifestation of strength and power. ...There is a quiet courage that comes from an inward spring of confidence in the meaning and significance of life. ...It has neither trumpet to announce it nor crowds to applaud; it is best seen in the lives of men and women who do their work from day to day without hurry and without fever. It is the patient waiting of the humble whose integrity keeps their spirit sweet and heart strong. Whenever one encounters it, a lift is given to life and vast reassurance invades the being. To walk with such a person is to keep company with angels."[39]

Where does that quiet kind of courage we need in the more ordinary days come from? How do we get it?

The naturalist writer Loren Eiseley may offer one answer in his description of an experience that began when he was hiking along Missouri's Platte River. At the edge of the river, where ice had formed, he looked down and saw a catfish frozen solidly in the ice. "Whatever sunny dream had kept him paddling there while the mercury plummeted downward and that Cheshire smile froze slowly, it would be hard to say," Eiseley writes. He started to turn away, but out of some impulse to test the survival qualities of high-plains fishes, he "blocked him out of the ice as gently as possible and dropped him, ice and all, into a collecting can in the car. Eiseley was tired by the time he arrived home, so he just set the can in the basement and went to bed. The next day, however, to his amazement, he discovered the fish swimming in the melted water in the can. As he tells it, the fish was saying, "Get me a tank."

"This was no Walden pickerel," Eiseley writes. "This was a yellow-green, mud-grubbing, evil-tempered inhabitant of floods and droughts and cyclones. It was the selective product of the high continent and the waters that pour across it. It had outlasted prairie blizzards that left cattle standing frozen upright in the drifts."

He said to himself, "I'll get the tank."

Eiseley and the fish lived together all that winter. "In the spring," Eiseley writes, "a migratory impulse or perhaps sheer boredom struck him. Maybe, in some little lost corner of his brain, he felt, far off, the pouring of the mountain waters through the sandy coverts of the Platte. Anyhow, something called to him, and he went. One night when no one was about, he simply jumped out of his tank. I found him dead on the floor next morning. He had made his gamble like a man—or, I should say, a fish. In the proper place it would not have been a fool's gamble. Fishes in the drying shallows of intermittent prairie streams who feel their confinement and have the impulse to leap while there is yet time may regain the main channel and survive to spawn another day.

"A million ancestral years had gone into that jump, I thought as I looked at him, a million years of climbing through prairie sunflowers and twining in and out through the pillared legs of drinking mammoths.

"I missed him," Eiseley continues. "He had for me the kind of lost archaic glory that comes from the water brotherhood. We were both projections out of that timeless ferment and locked as well in some greater unity that lay incalculably beyond us."

He then concludes, "There is no logical reason for the existence of a snowflake any more than there is for nature, that final world which contains—if anything contains—the explanation of men and catfish and green leaves."[40]

I don't know where courage comes from, but I suspect it may be as deeply imbedded in us as it was for that yellow-green evil-eyed catfish. Neuroscientists are saying there may be an "archival survival circuit" hard-wired in our brains that automatically kicks in when fear is triggered in us. So it may be with courage. Somewhere deep within our very nature is the strength, the wisdom, the vision to struggle and go beyond what we might know possible to uncover what it takes to do what we do.

The theologian Paul Tillich, from whom the title of this essay was taken, may be saying something similar when he says true courage comes not from within, but from beneath and beyond; it comes from being itself. Our very being, that which creates us and that which we create, contains what we need to move us forward.

But I come primarily not to discuss with you where this courage comes from but more to honor it. Courage is the bedrock of the religious journey. It is where life confronts what would dissolve it, or would make it false, or meaningless, or fearful, or dishonest. Saying yes in the face of life is the ultimate religious call.

"If you read history," writes my colleague Bill Zelazny, "one thing that seems to stand out is that armies lose battles, and businesses fail when their leaders take them too far—when they try to do more than they are able to do with the resources they have.

"On the other hand, history also shows us that sometimes things are not done, which could have been accomplished, because people were too timid. To try to do too much, or to fail to start something because of timidity are both ways we give in to the no's—the no of 'you aren't good enough unless you do more,' and the no of 'don't do anything because you can only do something small.'"

My friend Robyn was a Unitarian Universalist, a mother of two young boys, and the director of the Planned Parenthood affiliate in Ann Arbor until her untimely death from cancer several years ago. Her office was a regular object of hate and violence. The building had been redone so that barricades protected those inside. Robyn was the one who had been trained and was responsible for facing the bombs.

More than once she had to clear the building while she searched the premises for some explosive or other destructive device. Only a few weeks before she died, she was called in to the office because a suspicious package had arrived. It was a small box wrapped in brown paper, the address scratched on with an uneven scrawl and sealed with strips of tape and no return address. The bomb squad was there when she arrived and they wanted to know what to do.

"I had to decide, should we open it?" she said to me and then, with tears in her eyes, "You know the hardest part was knowing that I hadn't said goodbye to my kids and what if it had gone off?"

I do not know where Robyn's courage ultimately came from, but I know that she so believed in what she did that she could not stop doing it, no matter how scary it was. Fortunately, there was no bomb in that package. Just one more hoax. But to this day her courage continues to encourage me and many.

Maybe that is it for me. Courage comes when we need to be faithful to what we most believe in. It comes when we know we can do no other. It is out of courage that hope comes.

"To be hopeful in bad times," writes historian Howard Zinn, "is not just foolishly romantic. It is based on the fact that human history is a history not only of cruelty, but also of compassion, sacrifice, courage, kindness.

"What we choose to emphasize in the complex history will determine our lives. If we see only the worst, it destroys our capacity to do something. If we remember those times and places— and there are so many—where people have behaved magnificently this gives us the energy to act, and at least the possibility of sending this spinning top of a world in a different direction.

"And if we do act, in however small a way we don't have to wait for some grand utopian future. The future is an infinite succession of presents, and to live now as we think human beings should live, in defiance of all that is bad around us, is itself a marvelous victory."[41]

We are in the midst of incredible divisive and ugly political and practical bickering and one-up-man-ship. Those with wealth are running amuck with their power and influence. Governors in many states are grandstanding on the backs of the poor and elderly, not with goodness in mind, but pure self-interest as their guide.

The courage to be is the courage to say yes in the face of great or small no's like these we see around us. Our yes can move us toward a better tomorrow.

True spirituality does not ask us to put our trust or faith in a particular book or in a particular person. It asks us to have faith in ourselves arising out of our notion that we are of worth and dignity, we are of good stuff.[42] In confronting with courage all that life presents us is giving witness to that stuff. I am inspired by what many do, sometimes daily, sometimes with such integrity it causes me to take in a very deep breath of awe. I come to say, I honor their courage and the many ways they live it.

Questions for further reflection

1. Where does courage come from? How do you rate your courage quotient?
2. Can you name the ways you have been courageous? Or times you have failed to be courageous?

Of Things Spiritual

"I don't know beans about God," concludes writer Annie Dillard when she talks about things spiritual.

Dillard suggests that our spiritual journey may take years, picking up pieces of the truth along the way and also dropping some because there is no way of knowing with absolute certainty. The journey may or may not have anything to do with God. Spiritual seekers don't quit, Dillard writes. "They stick with it. Year after year they put one foot in front of the other, though they fare nowhere. Year after year they find themselves still feeling with their fingers for lumps in the dark."

For those who journey on a spiritual path, the path is enough. Certainty is not the center of that journey, but uncertainty may be. Doubt about what they know is a constant companion.

"I don't think life makes sense," writes theologian Sharon Welsh, "but I do know that there can be joy and wonder in the service of beauty and justice, and that may be a starting point to talk about things spiritual."

"May be" is a phrase used a lot by most of us who think about the spiritual life. Things spiritual are beyond our ever completely knowing, yet somehow we cannot stop the search simply because reason does not find a definitive answer. It is the mystery of life that sustains me now.

"There is within us a fundamental dis-ease, an unquenchable fire that renders us incapable, in this life, of ever coming to full peace," notes Ronald Rothheiser. This desire lies at the center of our lives, in the marrow of our bones, and in the deep recesses of the soul. At the heart of all great literature, poetry, art, philosophy, psychology, and religion lies the naming and analyzing of the desire. Spirituality is, ultimately, about what we do with that desire. What we do with our longings, both in terms of handling the pain and the hope they bring us, is our spirituality. ...Spirituality is about what we do with our unrest."[43]

Spirituality and religion are places for our unrest. Religions differ from the spiritual, however. Religion is associated with a brand, a particular kind, a place where spirituality is explored, found, and expressed. Religion helps us find peace as we struggle with fundamental human issues such as, "How do I live a generous and moral life?" and at the same time, "How do I follow my search for peace and security?" How do we balance this need for service to the larger community and for service to self?

No one religion fully answers these and other of our questions. We are on a journey, and no one faith tradition or discipline, including science, or psychology, or healing work, or meditation, will suffice. If we remain open to insights from what life delivers, we will discover that what was truth held five years ago is no longer true, or at least not as true. Not only books and the media bring us new insights, but if we are open to those around us who are living charitable and engaged lives, we can't help but see the world in new ways. As my knowledge has increased, my beliefs, my faith, and my spirituality has changed.

A spiritual path is found in all religions. It is not exclusive in its search, never stops seeking, and looks in places near and far for clues and pointers, but does not believe the answer is finally found.

I wonder if this is something of what Jesus had in mind when he spoke of the Kingdom of Heaven being like a mustard seed, small in its beginnings but becoming much changed as it grows (Matthew 3:31–32).

In a series of letters, author Elizabeth Lesser and religious historian Huston Smith compare and argue ideas about religion and spirituality. In one note, Ms. Lesser writes: "I once heard you [Smith] compare the human being to a lantern that contains within it the flame of the divine. You said, 'A lantern may have a functioning light within it, but it may be coated with dust and soot, sometimes even with mud. Sometimes the light does not shine through at all. Religious practice helps the faithful clean the surface of the lantern; that is what all the great traditions are for—to help us remove the dross that conceals divinity, so that the light can shine through.'

"I agree with you," Ms. Lesser continues. "In fact, I think you may have defined the purpose of all spiritual life—to clean the surface of the lantern."[44]

These two argue that our spiritual life is internal, a mystery that lies within and yet it is not fully known, nor can it be simply or automatically understood or felt, but is fundamental to religious faith.

We should cultivate for ourselves a special kind of understanding or knowing, as Ralph Waldo Emerson suggested, a knowing in the spirit of things. This kind of knowing is a personal experience and knowledge of a divine presence that can be described, but not explained. It is a kind of inner knowing that goes before reason or logic. I find it helpful to say we can describe but not explain the nature of the spiritual life.

I compare this to what Dr. Smith describes as discovering the spiritual as an inward journey. Religious truth, psychotherapy, physical self-healing, and meditation are all paths toward what he calls the light or what we know as our spiritual guide. This spirituality may be hiding out amid the obvious. Cleaning the surface of the lantern is a metaphor for that deep and abiding wisdom discovered as we search our innermost self where the spiritual is found. It may be an intense journey, yet one that demands each of us take responsibility for our own reverence, our own virtue, our own ethic of love and service.

"At this point in my life I don't believe in God," writes Professor Welsh. "I know of no concepts, symbols, or images of God, goddess, gods, or divinity that I find intellectually credible, emotionally satisfying, or ethically challenging in the face of evil and the complexity of life. I do know, however, of spiritual practices that do change our lives, that help us see where we are wrong, that propel us to work for justice, that provide a sense of meaning and joy. For my parents and their community, such solace and challenge could be found in daily prayer, in preparing and giving sermons, in individual and collective study and worship, and in physical work with other people—building cabins at the church campgrounds, cooking, cleaning, working together on the concrete tasks that sustain us physically."

As Annie Dillard said, this spirituality business is a too big, too mysterious thing. The spiritual may be much simpler than we imagine. She suggests further, "We live in all we seek. The hidden shows up in too-plain sight. It lives captive in the face of the obvious—the people, events, and the things of the day—to which we as sophisticated children have long since become oblivious. What a hideout: Holiness lies spread and borne over the surface of time and stuff like color."[45]

The spiritual lies in the midst of life, woven into the fabric of the everyday. The holy may be spread all about us like color. Cynthia Ginsburg sells stocks and bonds. In the midst of the loss of her mother to breast cancer and starting a new career she found a therapist, but to that she added Jewish meditation retreats, engaged in yoga practice, studied philosophy and came to understand that her whole life is spiritual practice. "To be on a spiritual path," she writes, "means to me that actions count, thoughts count, everything matters."

Perhaps there is no one definition of the spiritual that ever completely satisfies, and yet it is lived out in a variety of ways. Recently, the actress Angelina Jolie received the United Nations Humanity Award for her work with refugees in Ghana and elsewhere around the world. In an interview, she noted that there are a half-million hungry, homeless refugees in Ghana alone and millions more in other corners of the world and she was driven to try to make some kind of difference.

In the midst of such overwhelming numbers, the incredible odds of making a difference seem puny indeed. I stare at these people awash in suffering and I pause to ask, "What in the world do I do? Who in the world am I to make any difference?" Those, I believe, are the questions we ask because our very being asks them of us. In the midst of these questions about suffering humanity, the spiritual is our guide and makes life count for something.

"For me," writes Dr. Welsh, "the [spiritual] purposes of awareness and gratitude are served through meditation, dance, hearing live music, teaching ethics, and, like my parents, manual labor with and for other people. Spiritual openness may be sustained by intense physical activity and evoked by meditative awareness. These practices do not guarantee, however, that we will act justly. Profound experiences of connection and spiritual ecstasy can easily fuel self-righteous certainty and exclusivity. But these same experiences may also provide the connections with other people and with nature that motivate us to work for justice, honoring that nature, those people we respect. These practices can enable us to learn where we are wrong in our strategies and actions, can teach us to learn from criticism, and help us to gain the courage to act on our ideals."

Spiritual practice is the chance to live out the best of one's talents in response to nature, to people, to the particular opportunities for beauty and justice in one's immediate world. Spirituality brings us into full engagement with the world around us. It takes what we too easily believe to be our puny insignificant selves and gives us purpose.

Because we are human, we will make false starts and mistakes on the search, and at times the religious traditions will hinder rather than help, because they can obscure rather than enlighten.

I often ask, "How do I know what is the right path? Why do I choose to live in such a way that my choices take me in one direction and not another?" At the end of the day, it may be that I am guided by an inner light and I can know no more than that. This spiritual guide has grown out of the teachings of my elders, my church, my friends and my experiences. I know the path to take because this inner voice, this spiritual guide now points the way.

Questions for further reflection

1. What does it mean to say spirituality and religion are places for our unrest? Are not they places of comfort and peace?
2. Dr. Welsh writes that "the [spiritual] purposes of awareness and gratitude are served through meditation, dance, hearing live music, teaching ethics, and, like my parents, manual labor with and for other people. Is this true or is she being too general to be helpful?

Our Missteps on Race

The bananas would come flying out of the stands and land on the soccer field. Brendan Batson can still recall the monkey chants, with fans grunting in unison every time he and his two black teammates touched the ball.

That was the experience of many black soccer players in "the bad old days," as they call them now. Yet today almost every country in Europe has racist signs, chants, and even violence at soccer stadiums, particularly from rightist groups that single out blacks, Jews, Muslims, or other ethnic groups for ridicule. Some demonstrators say they do it only to unsettle the opposing team, but the evidence is that hatreds go much deeper.

A blatant example of prejudice chants came when England played Slovakia in a qualifying round for the 2004 European championships. A portion of the Slovak fans chanted "ooo-ooo-ooo" at two black English players.

"When I went to pick up the ball," one of the offended players said, "even the stretcher staff was making monkey chants."[46]

Such racist behavior occurs in Italy, Spain, Austria, Poland, and the Netherlands. I report such incidents because as I read of them I am aware that racist behavior is not only found in the United States. It appears to be part of the human condition. Perhaps we have evolved in competition with each other, and our negative and sometimes cruel behavior toward one another goes as far back as our very early beginnings as human beings.

For generations the Pequot, the Massachusetts, Nauset, and Narraganset tribes cultivated corn and learned to let fields lie fallow every third year so they would be renewed. After the harvest celebration, the tribes would distribute money, coats, and knives to the poor. Often they gave corn to the Pilgrims to sustain them through the cold Eastern shore winters. They hunted, fished, cleared and farmed the land, and like others, sometimes were cruel and fought with each other.

While the Indians were harvesting and hunting in North America, the British were colonizing Ireland. There Protestant landowners converted the peasants' land from farming to grazing for cattle production. The process displaced more than ninety percent of the Irish farmers, who had to live on potatoes and buttermilk so beef could be exported to England. About that time, a little known fungus destroyed about forty percent of the potato crop, and in the next ten years famine killed one million Irish. One and a half million who survived left their homeland for the United States.

Those Irish immigrants provided the labor for the construction of roads and canals for the growing market economy that was driving America's expansion. Standing knee deep in water and cursing swarms of mosquitoes, they built the Erie in New York, the Blackstone in Rhode Island, and the Enfield in Connecticut. They also built the Western and Atlantic Railroad from Atlanta to Chattanooga and the Union Pacific segment of the transcontinental. They were the hands and backs of the growing shoe and garment factories, and maids in the kitchens, laundries, and dining rooms. Gradually they became the skilled tradesmen, the steamfitters, the teamsters, the steel workers and stonecutters.

That railroad the Irish were building westward led not only to American expansion toward Asia, but brought the migration of Asians to America. A few years before the Civil War, a U.S. policy maker, Aaron Palmer, proposed that Chinese laborers be imported to build the railroad east and to bring California land under cultivation. Many came, some to be free of the conflicts caused by the Opium Wars, or from the floods that had destroyed their land, or from the poverty imposed by the Qing government's policy of heavy taxation. Labor brokers distributed leaflets announcing: "Americans are very rich people. They want the Chinaman to come and make him very welcome. There you will have great pay, large houses, and food and clothing of the finest discription [sic]."

Most of them paid their own way, others borrowed from relatives, and many left wives and family behind. Some came in the Gold Rush of 1849 and settled mostly in California, but others went to Montana, Idaho, and New England.

Many who had been farmers in China drained California swamps and constructed miles of irrigation dikes and ditches that transformed farms from wheat to fruit. They taught their white employers how to plant, cultivate, and harvest orchard and garden crops. In the Salinas Valley, their labor increased the value of the land from $28 an acre to $100 an acre in just two years.

They opened laundries. With only a few dollars they could begin, and by drawing a circle for a dime or a larger circle for fifty cents they could manage without knowing numbers or much English. They built Chinatowns in Sacramento, and Marysville and Stockton, cities where their labor was in demand.

Some sought their fortunes working the mines and organized their own small companies. But the phrase "doesn't stand a Chinaman's chance" comes from the reality that after their mining claims were stolen from them by white settlers, the Chinese had little hope of ever recovering what was theirs.

The mines wore out, so thousands left to join other Chinese on the railroad. When white workers demanded the company stop hiring the Chinese, the superintendent replied: "We can't get enough white labor to build this railroad, and build it we must, so we're forced to hire them."

By 1862, Chinese made up ninety percent of the railroad's entire work force and the Central Pacific was their achievement. The famous photographs of the joining of the rail lines from East and West do not include Chinese faces. They were ordered out of the pictures.

While the Chinese were building a railroad in America, Commodore Matthew Perry sailed his navy ships into Tokyo Bay and forced open Japan's doors to the West. In fear of colonization similar to the British in China, the Japanese instituted a program of industrialization and militarization, financed by heavy taxes. That taxation fell hard on farmers and many, unable to pay, were forced to sell their property. Those facing hunger and poverty opted to travel west, many landing in Hawaii and the West Coast of the United States.

As skilled farmers, they converted marginal land in the San Joaquin, Sacramento and Imperial valleys of California into some of the most productive in the west. Some harvested crops as migrants; others caught salmon on fishing boats for canneries and loaded heavy ties to build the railroads.

Beginning the 1600s, long before the Japanese and Chinese came to California, an extensive line of Spanish and Mexican military officers helped establish the missions and the colonization of the five hundred miles from Mexico north toward Los Angeles, Santa Barbara, Monterey, San Jose, San Francisco and Sonoma. Settlers in these areas were mostly from Mexico, poor by any standard, and sent to the area with the promise of a good life. They were expected to settle and develop the land. Don Vallejo was one of those who succeeded and by the 1840s had accumulated 175,000 acres where he raised cattle and developed one of the most complete libraries on the west coast.

At the turn of the twentieth century, the poverty of Mexico drove many to find work in the cotton and beet fields from

California to Michigan and in hotels as waiters and elevator men from Texas to New York. In the middle 1920s, more than a quarter of the construction workers in Texas were Chicanos. They worked in the steel mills of Bethlehem, Pennsylvania, and as seamstresses in Los Angeles. "We couldn't [manage our agriculture] if we didn't have their labor," said an official of the San Antonio Chamber of Commerce.

The Jews also came at the turn of the century, only they came to the Lower East Side of New York to escape the pogroms in Russia. In their intense desire to become American, they first were peddlers and then established garment factories that revolutionized the way clothes were made.

I share these pieces of history as a reminder of the diversity that has made us who we are. In his fine book on multicultural America, Professor Ronald Takaki, writes:

"The signs of America's ethnic diversity can be discerned across the continent—Ellis Island, Angel Island, Chinatown, Harlem, South Boston, the Lower East Side, places with Spanish names like Los Angeles, and San Antonio or Indian names like Massachusetts and Iowa. Much of what is familiar in America's cultural landscape actually has ethnic origins. The Bing Cherry was developed by an early Chinese immigrant named Ah Bing. American Indians were cultivating corn, tomatoes, and tobacco long before the arrival of Columbus." Although there is uncertainty about it's origins, Dr. Takaki suggests that "the term *okay* was derived from the Choctaw word *oke*, meaning 'it is so.' There is evidence" he continues, "indicating that the name *Yankee* came from Indian terms for the English. Jazz and blues as well as rock and roll have African-American origins. The 'Forty-Niner' of the Gold Rush learned mining techniques from the Mexicans; American cowboys acquired herding skills from Mexican *vaqueros* and adopted their range terms—such as *lariat, lasso,* and *stampede.* Songs like 'God Bless America,' 'Easter

Parade,' and 'White Christmas' were written by a Russian-Jewish immigrant named Israel Baline, more popularly known as Irving Berlin." [47]

A history of these United States is not complete without the stories of the accomplishments of those who have or continue to suffer the slings and arrows of discrimination, racism, and poverty. Yet they have all been a vital part of creating this nation. There is more to their story, and it begins very early.

Around the year 1,000 AD, a small band of those Indians who were cultivating corn and tomatoes here watched as a floating island pulled by billowy clouds unloaded a group of strangers carrying long shiny sticks. They had never seen such people—hairy and pale skinned, blue eyed, and hair the color of the sun. Confused and frightened, the Indians hid beneath their skin-covered boats hoping to appear like three mounds on the beach. They heard the footsteps coming toward them, then suddenly their boats were overturned. All but one of them was captured. The lone survivor paddling away looked back to see his companions' blood staining the beach.

The leader of that expedition was Thorvold Ericson, who had sailed from Greenland to the New World. After the massacre, Ericson made camp on the beach with the promise that he would establish his home there. It was not to be. That night he and his men were attacked by Indians, and Ericson was killed.

From the very first encounters, white European males descended on the inhabitants of this land, and many other lands, and killed and destroyed them. It was a tragic pattern too often repeated throughout history.

Years later, in 1790, descendants of other white Europeans passed a law called the Naturalization Act, which prohibited non-white immigrants from becoming citizens, even the Indians who were here long before those white men ever arrived. That law was not repealed until 1952, long after Chicanos picked and carted and shipped beets and tomatoes and cotton so others might live; after the Japanese were interred in U.S. concentration camps, like Manzanar, for no other reason than that they were Japanese; long after the railroad blocked food to its Chinese workers because they were demanding the same pay as whites doing the same work; long after African-Americans had not only given their lives in the Civil War, but had suffered segregated conditions during World War I and II where they were decorated numerous times for bravery; long after Indians found that the land they had settled was taken away by law and Supreme Court rulings; long after the Irish and Jews, under sometimes deadly conditions in garment factories, had made the clothes that kept others protected in winter and summer.

Those diverse multitudes, African-American, Irish, Jewish, Japanese, Chinese, Mexican, Filipino, Portuguese, and almost any other immigrant group, labored to develop this country, died fighting for a democratic America, and suffered the oppression that seems to come with being different from white European.

The United States government has held or continues to hold hundreds of prisoners in camps such as Abu Ghraib, Guantánamo, and lesser known but equally vile settings, with no rights and often suffering indescribable abuse, even death. Recently the U.S. Supreme Court ruled without comment that people sent to foreign countries and injured and tortured by illegal interrogation and detention would not be allowed their day in a U.S. court.[48]

We can feel powerless to confront or change the wrongs in our society, but as Professor Derrick Bell writes, "Our lives gain purpose and worth when we recognize and confront the evils we encounter—small as well as large—and meet them with determination to take action even when we are all but certain that our efforts will fail. For in rising to these challenges, there is no failure. Rather there is the salvation of spirit, of mind, of soul."[49]

In creating a better world, we risk not getting it right, but risk we must to confront the evils that beset us. To create better communities means giving voice to all by including all in the history we tell for these are the stories we tell of ourselves.

E Pluribus Unum, "from many one," is our motto, but that motto has never been truly lived out. There have always been groups who have never been fully included in the mainstream, whatever that is. As Professor Takaki reminds us, "America's dilemma has been our resistance to ourselves—our denial of our immensely varied selves. But we have nothing to fear but our fear of our own diversity."

We have made important strides toward healing a diverse and divided society and we have looked at the ways discrimination has caused untold suffering, but we have yet to eradicate from our national systems and our lives the use of power that creates inequity rather than cooperation.

"Community does not mean 'free of conflict,'" writes author and poet Mary Phifer. "It's inevitable and even healthy to have great differences. Even conflict can lead to closeness. A strong community will include people of different ages, ethnic backgrounds, socioeconomic status, and interests. Community, communication, and communal come from the same word, meaning 'together' and 'next to.' Embedded in the world is the concept of shared place."

In difference we are enriched and learn more of who we truly are.

Questions for further reflection

1. Reflect on your family's history and lineage. What parts of the world have contributed to your ancestry?
2. How do the differences you experience in your life enrich your experience and self-knowledge?

It's About...Well, Err...Ummm

Slow down.
Is that you?
Feed me.
I want.
"If your vagina could talk, what would it say, in two words?"
Yum. Yum.
Oh, yeah.
Start again.
No, over there.
Lick me.
Stay home.
Brave choice.
Think again.
More, please.
Embrace me.
Let's play.
Don't stop.
More, more.
Remember me?
Come inside.
Not yet.
Whoa, Mama.
Yes yes.
Rock me.
Enter at your own risk.
Oh, God.
Thank God.
I'm here.

Let's go.

Find me.

Thank you.

Bonjour.

Too hard.

Don't give up.

Where's Brian?

That's better.

Yes, there. There.

Eve Ensler, who wrote those words, has helped us all on a journey of truth telling, of saying the unsayable. She helps us move beyond the part we talk about and the part we don't. And as Gloria Steinem writes in the introduction to Ensler's *The Vagina Monologues*, the central ceremony of patriarchal religions is one in which men take over the power of creation. Male religious leaders perpetuate the notions that humans were born in sin—because we were born to female creatures, a la, another Eve. "Only by obeying the rules of the patriarchy can we be reborn through men. No wonder priests and ministers in skirts sprinkle imitation birth fluid over our heads, give us new names, and promise rebirth into everlasting life. No wonder the male priesthood tries to keep women away from the altar, just as women are kept away from control of our own powers of reproduction. Symbolic or real, it's all devoted to controlling the power that resides in the female body."

Sex abounds, indeed. And so do sexual images, and both sexual repression and sexual exploitation in schools, the media, literature, and advertising. While flooded by sexual images on movie and television screens, male viewers are called scoundrels for looking. Human sexuality is considered a private matter. One's sexual orientation, habits, behavior are deeply personal and do not easily lend themselves to public debate. Nevertheless, sex ought to be out of the closet and into our conversations, guided by wisdom, insight, and care for the listener's ability to hear and understand. Thank you Eve Ensler for helping us get there.

Which brings me to Mr. and Mrs. Simpson, who had tried everything, but who had failed, in spite of many attempts, to have children. Finally, their doctor said, "Listen, there is absolutely no physiological reason why you should not have children. It is undoubtedly a matter of tension. You're trying too hard. Go home and forget the whole thing. Don't take temperatures, don't worry about the time of the month. Just live as normal a life as possible without concern for procreation. If on any occasion, however, you should have the impulse to have sex, then don't wait. Follow your instincts."

Some months later, Mrs. Simpson was back in the doctor's office and the tests showed that she was indeed pregnant. "Did you follow my advice?" the doctor asked.

"Yes, we did doctor, and it worked," Mrs. Simpson replied. "We lived a normal, carefree life, and then one evening at dinner, I dropped my napkin. I bent to pick it up and so did my husband. Our fingers touched beneath the table and it was like an electric shock going through the two of us. We remembered what you said, and we just stopped in the middle of dinner and made love under the table. And that's when I got pregnant."

"I'm delighted," the doctor said, "and I can imagine just how pleased you are."

"Completely happy, doctor, except for one thing. The maitre'd won't let us into the restaurant anymore."

There are times when it seems that our sexuality drives us, rather than the other way around. We are sexual beings, created in part to perpetuate the species, and that drive, for most of us, becomes too strong to resist as well as a delightful pleasure.

Our conversations, discussions, and teaching about sex are, at times, distorted and limited by those in society who would have us keep the topic a private, family matter. The darkness that surrounds our sexual lives is not just what we do in the dark, but also what we keep out of the light of discussion and public reflection.

The late Robert Maplethorpe must be laughing at the likes of Orin Hatch, the American Family Association, and others who would limit and define the conversation about human sexuality to what they deem appropriate. A few years ago, detractors of Maplethorpe's photographic prints of sexually explicit images, including whips, leather, and fists and fingers in unusual places sought to close down his exhibit at the Cincinnati Contemporary Arts Center. The Center, however, refused to be intimidated and stood firm in its right to exhibit what it believed to be fine art.

Some of Maplethorpe's vision I find unappealing, offensive, and perhaps sensational for the sake of sensation. I also find that censoring such art stifling to the creative process. John Frohnmayer was fired as head of the National Endowment of the Arts for his support of Maplethorpe and the Museum's right to exhibit what it felt was fine art. At the time, Frohnmayer said, "The arts communicate to us before they are understood." And so it is. Great art helps us see and understand the world in new ways. It will be misunderstood for it is ahead of us. Censorship of such only hinders our ability to see in new ways. To conclude in advance that what is depicted by the artist is evil, obscene, or wrong when what it may be communicating we do not yet understand limits our growth. We may decide some artists' work is not for us, or that it ought not be viewed by children, or is even dangerous, but we ought to determine for ourselves what is great art. Such choices should not be left to politicians and clergy.

There is some clearly marked evidence of pornography where the persons depicted have been coerced into acts or poses they would not otherwise agree to, or when violence is used against participants and persons are used in demeaning, dangerous, or dehumanizing poses or activities. The erotic, on the other hand, includes persons depicted in relationships, and the material suggests pleasure, not pain, and foreplay, kissing, massage, mutual undressing, softness, vulnerability, intimacy.

The erotic is of our nature, part of being whole. The photographer Duane Michaels writes, "What is this want that makes me turn to look at you? I do not know. It is of me as is my breath. Do you tell yourself to breathe? It is my nature, and being nature is not right or wrong or good or bad, but innocent of purpose. It is my body's music and its truth. And I become a queer and peculiar thing, out of harmony, when I silence my song because you find it inappropriate."

Our sexuality is part of our song, for all of our lives. It changes as we age. It matures as we mature. So it was for a woman of advanced years who anxiously went to a psychiatrist. "Doctor," she said, "I have a problem. My husband is losing his potency and I am anxious to discover if the condition is psychological or if the cause is physical."

The psychiatrist was taken back and asked, "How old are you madam?"

"Eighty," was her reply.

The psychiatrist scratched his head and then asked, "and how old is your husband?"

"Eighty-three."

Now the psychiatrist seemed stumped. He brooded a bit and tried again. "Well, when did you first notice he was losing his potency?"

"Oh, I first noticed it last night, but what troubles me is that I noticed it again this morning."

Our understanding of our sexuality is changing in part due to the work of feminist scholars, including Sharon Welsh and

Carol Gilligan. Both have pioneered in helping us understand how men and women see the world differently, and as Gilligan reports, "Women's place in man's life cycle has been that of nurturer, caretaker, and helpmate, the weaver of those networks of relationships on which she in turn relies. But while women have thus taken care of men, men have, in their theories of psychological development, as in their economic arrangements, tended to assume or devalue that care. When the focus on individuation and individual achievement extends into adulthood and maturity is equated with personal autonomy, concern with relationships appears as a weakness of women rather than as a human strength."[50]

Women have known what men are beginning to discover, that intimacy, relationships, and caring are vital, fundamental to human growth and wholeness. For women, morality is based on the elaboration of what makes relationships work and help and heal. What Freud and others have led us to believe is that doing and living by what builds relationships is morally insufficient. Morality built on what is best for the individual, as men often see it, is seen by some psychoanalysts as a higher form of moral development. The irony is that women's understanding has led us toward a kind of morality based not on the primacy and universality of individual rights, but rather on what Gilligan describes as a "very strong sense of being responsible to the world."[51]

Gilligan and others have helped us see sex in context. Sex is attraction. Sex is connection. Sex is joyful play. Sex is intense, fulfilling, and bonding. Sex can also be abusive, and controlling, and painful. Sex is our creation, a way of being with another. How we are together ranges from playful and joyous to vengeful and painful.

It is in relationships where sex is made most real, in relationships where love and caring and intimacy are shared. I therefore digress for a moment to remind us of sex in context, by sharing a story from Rabbi Kushner:

"I was sitting on a beach one summer day, watching two children, a boy and a girl, playing in the sand. They were hard at work building an elaborate sand castle by the water's edge, with gates and towers and moats and internal passages. Just when they had nearly finished their project, a big wave came along and knocked it down, reducing it to a heap of wet sand. I expected the children to burst into tears, devastated by what had happened to all their hard work. But they surprised me. Instead, they ran up the shore away from the water, laughing, and holding hands, and sat down to build another castle. I realized that they had taught me an important lesson. All the things in our lives, all the complicated structures we spend so much time and energy creating, are built on sand. Only our relationships to other people endure. Eventually, the wave will come along and knock down what we have worked so hard to build up. When that happens, only the person who has somebody's hand to hold will be able to laugh."

Some of what we see about us these days between men and men and women and women and men and women is absurd, unlovely. The illogical, the unreasonable are clear enough. Yet, we also see about us caring relationships that are more powerful than the absurd, the unlovely, the mean. Love that is celebrated, cherished, and offered, as best we can, has the power to transform.

Love. No two of us know it the same way, or do it alike. Each of us knows and experiences it differently. Some of us have never known it, as we believed it should be, like we've seen it in the movies or read about it on Hallmark cards. Some of us have not known parents who loved us unconditionally, or even much at all. Some of us have had our love returned, empty.

Love. We seek it. We yearn for it. Some get it, some never do. Some give it who have never gotten it, some can't give it who have been given lots of it. For those who have not experienced love from parents or lovers, as well as for all who have, love emerges; it is created by reaching out and risking.

"There is no guarantee, that love will yield both happiness and meaning," writes philosopher Irving Singer. "The pursuit of love provides meaning in life, but the experience of it varies greatly in the quantity and quality of the happiness that results."[52]

Love. At the end of the day, it isn't what love *is* that we wonder about, it's whether we'll get enough of it, if any at all. In thinking about all this, I read about the biology of love. I learned that men aren't the only creatures to make dinner dates; black-tipped flies and road runners also offer food to their dates, in hopes of receiving sexual favors. I learned that flirtatious women who toss their hair and cock their heads are repeating a gambit that's millions of years old, that female opossums and mud turtles engage in similar displays. I learned that human beings share a taste for French kissing similar to a type of chimpanzee. Some, I learned, say love is simply biology. I even read a book on love by an MIT philosophy professor. It doesn't get much more erudite that that. In all of this I understood what the books said, but was left disappointed. What we want is not the biological or the philosophical or psychological rational for love. We want to be able to do more than know about love; we want to experience it. We want it to be real. Books can tell us about it. We must risk offering it to receive it.

What psychologists and psychiatrists have discovered is that attachment, the need to be connected to another, is buried deep in the primal part of our brain. It penetrates the core of what it means to be a human being. Laboratory experiments have shown that puppies separated from their mothers protest, and prolonged separations lead to despair. "Anyone who has been jilted in an infatuation," writes psychiatrist Thomas Lewis and others, "has experienced the protest...the inner restless-ness, the powerful urge to contact the person. ...The drive to reestablish contact is sufficiently formidable that people of-ten cannot resist it, even when they understand that the other person doesn't want anything to do with them. Human beings manifest searching and calling in lengthy letters, frantic phone calls, repeated emails, and telephoning an answering machine just to hear another's voice."[53]

At the heart of human sexuality is the call to be connected. It is hardwired into our brains. Dr. Rachel Remen describes a homeless woman whose visits to her doctor were complicated by her need to take with her all of her worldly possessions in a shopping cart, which she lashed to parking meters, one at a time, and hauled it up a steep San Francisco hill to his office. Her doctor treated her so kindly that this woman would return to his office even though she had no appointment and he was not there. She returned, it seems, to perform a simple ritual that somehow connected her to that doctor in that place. That was all she needed.

Dr. Remen then reminds us, "The places where we are genuinely met and heard have great importance to us. Being in them may remind us of our strength and our value in ways that many other places we may pass through do not. ...The places in which we are seen and heard are holy places. They remind us of our value as human beings. They give us the strength to go on." Those relationships where we are genuinely met are the places where our sexual natures are truly known and nurtured.

Questions for further reflection

1. Reflect on what love has meant in your life. Does it have anything to do with sex? Has it brought you joy, or disappointment, or loss?
2. Are there places in your life made holy by your being seen and heard?

Reflections on Enormous Events

A few days after the terrorist attack on the World Trade Center, I watched sculptor Richard Serra, who lives a few blocks away from the site, being interviewed as he and his neighbors tried to reconstruct their lives. "What are you going to do?" he was asked by a reporter. "I'm going to take out my garbage," he replied as he hauled two bags of trash to the curb.

We must go on with our lives, he was saying—but how? In these days of unprecedented tragedy and devastation in New York, New Orleans, Joplin, Missouri and elsewhere around the world, carrying on is what we do. I find myself overcome with a sense of helplessness, wanting to do something. But whatever I can do seems so miniscule compared to the enormity of the attacks and the violence of nature.

At the time of the attacks and in these days following the awesome revelation of nature's power, I find myself filled with a number of conflicting emotions. I felt anger at suicide bombers and perpetrators of such acts of violence. I was grief-stricken, mostly unable to even speak of the suffering that so many experienced. Much of what I felt was confusion and shock, and I suspect I am like those the *New York Times* reporter described earlier when he wrote, "Ground Zero remains the physical manifestation of our worst fears. We are still sorting out how to think about the long-term consequences of these horrific deeds."

On the Tuesday after the attack, I took a ladder and repaired the gutters that were filled with wet leaves and falling off my house—just to be doing something—with the growing sense that so much had and was happening around me that I could only watch, in horror, but do nothing to affect the outcome.

After the attacks, on Pat Robertson's religious TV program, *The 700 Club*, Baptist minister Jerry Falwell blamed the violence on pagans, abortionists, feminists, homosexuals, the American Civil Liberties Union, and the People for the American Way. "I point the finger in their face and say: You helped this happen," he said.

I suspect most of us would dismiss the Rev. Falwell as a religious fanatic using tragedy and pain to boost his ratings, as would Rev. Robertson. The reaction to his remarks were as they should be; firm, strong and to the point: "You are wrong, and stop it."

U.S. Secretary of Transportation Norman Mineta announced grimfaced on CNN that preparations and precautions were being made at U.S. airports in wake of the unspeakable terrorist attacks. "There will be no more curb-side parking at U.S. airports," he gravely intoned.

Now I bet that scared the bejesus out of Osama ben Laden and others who were sitting about their hideaway tables smiling, if not laughing out loud. It is not that Mr. Mineta was not doing what he could, but I must confess his response seemed about as effective or helpful as my own or others who simply were overwhelmed by the enormity of the events of those days.

At the time of the attacks, foreign affairs columnist for the *New York Times* Thomas Friedman made the convincing case that the Trade Center and Pentagon attacks were the Pearl Harbor of our day. We are not pitted against another superpower, as was the case in the Cold War of an earlier era, he writes. Rather we find our country pitted against super-empowered, very cunning, and angry men and women who do not share our values and resent our influence, power, and dominance in their lives. They have reason to hate the United States as they see it as the country that keeps them from a homeland of their own.

It was only a few steps from the destruction of the towers and the attack on the Pentagon for some to make the connection between piety and irony, when road shrines and public prayers were part of a great outpouring of uninhibited religiosity. George Bush quoted the 23rd Psalm and spoke of the United States' role in the conflict between good and evil. "We are embarked on a new kind of evil," he said, "and we understand, and the American people are beginning to understand, this crusade, the war on terrorism, is going to take a while."

Members of Congress sang "God Bless America" on the Capitol steps, and the war against Afghanistan was first called Operation Infinite Justice. As Jonathan Raban put it in a recent article in the *New York Review of Books*, "After September 11, America meant to play God in the world—not gentle Jesus, but wrathful, thunderous Jehovah."[54]

Although he wrote several years ago, professor Benjamin Barber could have been writing about the recent Iraq and Afganistan wars as well as the Trade Center attacks, by suggesting, "What we have seen is a war between the two eternities of race and soul," what he calls the Jihad versus the McWorld.[55] "There is," he writes, "on the one hand the grim prospect of a radicalization of large swaths of humankind by war and bloodshed: a threatened breaking up of nation-states in which culture is pitted against culture, people against people, tribe against tribe," what he calls "a Jihad in the name of a hundred narrowly conceived faiths against every kind of interdependence, every kind of artificial social cooperation and mutuality."

There are a growing number of people who seem to be "against technology, against pop culture and against integrated markets; against modernity itself."

On the other hand, Barber continues, "The McWorld paints the future in shimmering pastels; a busy portrait of onrushing economic, technological, and ecological forces that demand integration and uniformity that mesmerize people everywhere with fast music, fast computers, and fast food—MTV, Macintosh, and McDonalds—pressing nations into one homogenous global theme park, one McWorld tied together by communications, information, entertainment, and commerce."[56]

Barber concludes: "Jihad pursues a bloody politics of identity. McWorld, a bloodless economics of profit." The result is that we are living in a world where the leaders of this nation and followers of a radical religious ideology are willing to kill to have their values rule.

After months of poor performance and leadership, Michael Brown was removed by President Bush as head of the federal agency in charge of post-Katrina relief in New Orleans. While Bush didn't cite incompetence as the reason, most believe that Brown, who inflated his resume to get the job and who had no experience in emergency relief planning, was ill-suited for the Federal Emergency Management Agency post, to say the least. Here we see the president's ongoing appointments of his friends to high places regardless of their level of experience with matters over which they have responsibility. It's another example of how the world follows the path of profit rather than competence and compassion in policy and politics.

I admit to being a critic of how the relief efforts were handled in Katrina's wake, because I believe that the lives of hundreds of thousands were put at risk and given less than adequate care and support because the politics of the day put money and power above compassion for human life. There is a loss of respect for what many consider of highest priority: the worth and dignity of every person.

It should be noted that the people in Joplin, Missouri have reported that following the incredible hurricane devastation there where the worst tornado in 60 years has killed at least

122 and left thousands homeless and without food or shelter, that the Obama administration has responded admirably well.

The late Stephen Jay Gould describes standing at Ground Zero only a mile from his home, a day or so after the planes attacked the Twin Towers. He, his wife, and his stepdaughter established a depot to collect and ferry needed items in short supply, including respirators and shoe inserts, to the workers. People responded with everything from a pocketful of batteries to a ten-thousand-dollar purchase of hard hats, made on the spot at a local supply house.

Late one evening, as they left a local restaurant to make a delivery, the cook handed them a shopping bag and said, "Here's a dozen apple brown bettys, our best dessert, still warm. Please give them to the workers."

How lovely, Gould thought to himself, *but how meaningless, except as an act of solidarity, connecting the cook to the cleanup.* He had promised the delivery, however, and promised to make the distribution.

"Twelve apple brown bettys into the breach," he writes. "Twelve apple brown bettys for thousands of workers and then I learned something important that I should never have forgotten and the joke turned on me. Those twelve apple brown bettys went like literal hotcakes. These trivial symbols in my initial judgment turned into little drops of gold within a rainstorm of similar offerings for the stomach and soul, from children's postcards to cheers by the roadside. We gave the last one to a firefighter, an older man in a young crowd, sitting alone in utter exhaustion as he inserted one of our shoe pads. And he said, with a twinkle and a smile restored to his face: 'Thank you. This is the most lovely thing I've seen in four days—and still warm.'"[57]

Over against this simple act of decency and kindness, Jonathan Rabin offers a different picture that speaks of how far we have come since that September 11 attack: "I have lived in the U.S. for fifteen years," he writes, "and during the last four of those years, America, in its public and official face, has become more foreign to me by the day—which wouldn't be worth reporting, except that the sentiment is largely shared by so many Americans. The grammar and vocabulary of the language spoken by the administration and by a large part of the press differ so fundamentally from that spoken by people in my intellectual, political, and...geographical neighborhood that debate between the two has become like the Englishman's idea of speaking a foreign language, which is to shout ever more loudly in his own."[58]

I agree with Mr. Rabin, but I also remember Dr. Gould, who argues that patterns of human history mix decency and depravity, and that good and kind people outnumber all others by thousands to one. He notes, "In an important, little appreciated, and utterly tragic principle of nearly all complex systems, building up must be accomplished step by tiny step, whereas destruction need occupy but an instant. ...Ten thousand acts of kindness done by thousands of people, and slowly building trust and harmony over many years, can be undone by one destructive act of a skilled and committed psychopath. ...In reality, the decent multitudes, performing their ten thousand acts of kindness, vastly outnumber the very few depraved people in our midst. Thus, we have every reason to maintain our faith in human kindness, and our hopes for the triumph of human potential, if only we can learn to harness this wellspring of unstinting goodness in nearly all of us. "Thus," he concludes, "in what I like to call the Great Asymmetry, every spectacular incident of evil (or tragedy) will be balanced by ten thousand acts of kindness (or greatness), too often unnoted and invisible as the 'ordinary' efforts of a vast majority."

While we may not have easy solutions in the face of such overwhelming pain and suffering, we do have each other to offer love, comfort, financial and physical support, and strength. This is what we can do. Whatever we do, it sure beats my cleaning the gutters.

And so it is, that good deeds and good lives do so overwhelmingly outweigh the evil numbers and evil acts in our midst.

Questions for further discussion

1. Do you agree with Dr. Gould that the decent and caring people outnumber the depraved? Why?
2. How have the events of 9/11 affected you and the spirit of this country? Do you believe we are different people now than we were before the Trade Center attacks?

Rowing Together

Recently, I officiated at a memorial service where the church was crammed with standing room only of young, old, rich, poor, in a variety of colors and lifestyles. Some arrived in vans, sedans, and four-door coupes, while a large number rode in on Harley-Davidson motorcycles. They came dressed in suits and ties, dresses, blue jeans, and sweaters. Those who came on Harleys were dressed in leather and their jackets were inscribed with "The Brotherhood." They walked into the sanctuary in single file and stood at the back during the service. When the time came, one of them, with tears in his eyes, spoke to all of us gathered there. He told how the brothers cared for one another and how much they cared for the man we had come to honor. He spoke of community.

I might define community differently than The Brotherhood, not because their way is wrong, but rather because community has many wonderful ways of expressing itself.

A religious community is found where people share responsibility for the collective good. Each is his or her sisters' and brothers' keeper and embrace a vision of something larger than themselves. In such a community members are part of ritual, of joys and lamentation, of celebration of successes and the acknowledgment of our fallibility.

Community is the plural that we are in danger of losing to the cries for the singular. Indeed, community begins with one. It begins with the self. It begins with the acceptance of self as an incomplete whole, in need of others. As we grow in self-understanding however, we know we are complete only in connection with others, be it with three or four, or three or four hundred. Community begins with the self but ends in connection; moving toward a goal of a world community with peace, liberty, and justice for all. World community begins with one, but always with a larger vision in mind.

"It is only in community that we can find care," writes Professor John McKnight, in his book, *The Careless Society*. "It is only in community that we can hear people singing. And if you listen carefully, you can hear the words: 'I care for you, because you are mine, and I am yours.'"[59]

Rebecca Parker, the president of Starr King School for Ministry in California, tells of a man returning home: "At the end of World War II, Lyle Grunkenmeir came home to Iowa. In the small town he'd left to go the Western front, his mother and sisters waited for his return. The day he came home, the only veteran to return alive to that town, everyone came out to meet him. As the train pulled into the station the band played, the mayor was there to greet him.

"But his sister later told me, the man who climbed off the train was not the lively and cheerful boy who had left. The man who climbed off was a ghost. He didn't register recognition of any one—mother, sister, or friend. In response to the crowd's rousing welcome he stared blankly. He was mute.

"His family took him home to the farm. He sat in the old rocking chair in the parlor. He did not speak, or move, and would barely eat. He continued in this state for days that spilled into weeks that went on into months. No one in this town knew about traumatic shock. They only knew that Lyle's soul was lost somewhere.

"His sister, Maxine, decided to stay by him. Whenever she could, she would come and sit with him. And she would talk. She'd tell him about the church potluck, who was there, what they ate, what each young woman wore. She'd tell him about the conversation she'd overheard at the store in town and how high the crops were now. She told him how the wind, that day, had blown the clean laundry into the tomatoes. When she ran out of things to say, she would just sit with him, snapping beans, mending socks. And he sat there, silent, like a stone.

"Then one night, while she was sitting quietly with him, knitting, she looked over and saw that tears were falling from his eyes. She went to him, and put her arm around him. Then he began to cry full force, great sobs of anguish and bellowing from deep inside him. Then he began to talk and he would not stop. He talked of the cold, the fear, the noise, the death of his buddies, the long marches, and then, the human beings in the camps, the mass graves, the smell. He talked all night, until the dawn light began to creep across the fields and Maxine listened until he had told the whole story. Then she made him breakfast, and he went out and did the morning chores."[60]

Lyle Grunkenmeir's pain is being experienced countless numbers of times these days as our country continues to pursue its longest war that has long ago stopped making sense and now is running out of Lyle Grunkenmeirs to fight it. Instead, the broken down Walter Reed Hospital is filled to overflowing with more broken lives than it wants to handle and, ironically, is soon to be closed.

Judith Herman, a Harvard psychologist, has studied trauma and recovery. She suggests that there is a core event in each case of healing from trauma and that is that one human being stays with another human being until the numbed person is able to speak their silenced experiences.

"Healers," writes Henri Nouwen, "are hosts who patiently and carefully listen to the story of the suffering stranger."[61]

Healing comes as the story is spoken by one and witnessed by another who is able to listen to the pain and not run away. It requires that we not be our own back-scratcher; we need others to do it for us. It is a process that the contemplative Thomas

Merton says comes out of "the solitude of the heart." It is first listening to one's innermost self with compassion, with forgiveness, with acceptance. Then we can truly hear the other.

It is acceptance of self that precedes love of others, which then allows one listener to hear the pain of the injured, and there is a sense that they share a common core, the universal human connection. "It is because of deep solitude that I find the gentleness with which I can truly love [others]," writes Merton.

Without self love, or what Merton calls "deep solitude," our relationships with others become needy and greedy, sticky and clinging. Then our loneliness cries out to be rescued, and we are deaf to the needs of others. Love of self is where real community begins, for then we reach out not for our own good, but for the good of both. The singular becomes complete in the plural.

For those, like Lyle Grunkenmeir, for whom love of self is difficult or incomprehensible, it is the task of the community to care for them, just as his sister did, to offer love so it can be learned by those who believe they are unlovable.

Genuine religious community arises not as an alternative to the care of one's self. Rather, out of care of self comes the mandate to care for others. Out of caring for others comes community.

"The more solitary I am," Merton says, "the more affection I have for others. It is pure affection...filled with reverence for the well being of others."

Reverence for each other is the work of a liberal religious community. It means listening to our heart and acting from the heart.

In listening to the heart, we can truly hear the pains of the world because we recognize them not as strange and unfamiliar, but as pains that are indeed our own. That is not to suggest that we are responsible for all human suffering, but rather we are called to respond to it out of our solidarity with our fellow humans.[62]

The kind of community we seek to develop and make real requires both an inward and an outward look. It is as Anne Morrow Lindberg wrote: "We are all islands in a common sea."

The Rev. Scott Alexander tells of seventeenth-century Huguenots, a Protestant Reformation sect. Like so many other religious minorities of that time, they were relentlessly persecuted by the established church. Those who had not already been killed were finally forced to flee France altogether. One group of escapees jammed into a tiny boat and tried to row across the choppy and treacherous English Channel to safety.

As they began to row for their lives, it became painfully clear that there were just too many people in the boat. Unless something was done the small craft would soon swamp and all would perish beneath the cold waves. What would they do? They could draw lots and throw the losers overboard? They could set upon the defenseless sick, elderly, young. They could decide who were the least productive members of the community and force them out of the boat. They could have decided on any of these "rational" courses of action, but these beleaguered Huguenots did something far nobler. Without any wailing or whining, the people in the boat decided they would take turns—several at a time—swimming alongside the craft. For the many hours of the crossing, as swimmers tired, others would quietly, willingly take their place in the numbing waters—and thus it was that the small boat and everyone who had sought refuge in it—survived the treacherous crossing.[63]

Rowing together or being like Lyle Grunkenmeir's sister Maxine is the work of community where each one sustains all in the act of reaching out. It is a place where we listen to our heart and act on what we hear. It is looking inward and outward at the same time. I remind us of Thomas Merton's words: "It is because of deep solitude that I find the gentleness with which I can truly love [others], beginning with the love of self that grows to include others we build "a world community of love, justice and compassion."

Questions for further reflection

1. What is necessary for self love to exist? How can we make it happen?
2. Describe what community means to you. Is there any place where it exists for you?

On Sharing Umbrellas

I grew up in a middle- to upper-middle-class neighborhood and have lived and worked in such neighborhoods as well as down-and-out slums, and I have never found a satisfactory answer to the question Mary Gordon asks in her novel *Spending*. She asks, "How much beauty is enough, how much pleasure is enough?" Her question leads me to ask, "What is my relationship to money and its use? How much do I deserve, how much do I need for a good life, whatever that means?"

Monica Szabo is a middle-aged moderately successful painter who frequently reflects on a love affair and money, as Mary Gordon describes her in *Spending*. Monica's lover is identified only as B until the last page of the book. He is rich and offers to support her for two years so she can engage in her painting full-time. In considering their life, Monica notes:

"He took me to restaurants I'd never gone to and never would have gone to without him. ...Once he took me to Petrossian and we spent hundreds of dollars on caviar. Dollops of it were brought to us on silver platters. It seemed like something you'd only do once, so I thought, why not, why not, a bit of old Russia. ...You were paying to pretend you were in another time and place. But hundreds of dollars for a meal," I said, "it isn't worth it."

"Worth?" he said. "What's worth?"

"You have to have some sense of worth," she replied. "To the person who works at a hospital, a nurse's aide, minimum wage, the Argo Luncheonette on Ninetieth and Broadway is out of sight. Not worth it."

"I had to think about money in a new way," Monica continues. "It was simultaneously more abstract and more real than it had ever been. How much was too much when you had more than enough? In a world of desirables, what did you say no to? It was easy for me to make the decision for myself; a good use of money bought time for work, education, and freedom for my children, a certain amount of pleasure, attractive food, someplace to live that didn't look like Lee Harvey Oswald was brought up there, an occasional new item of clothing. I've never been tempted by purchases that were supposed to announce who I was in the world: the right brand of this or that. Of course, everything you buy says something about who you are. ...

"I started trying to understand the idea of luxury. Something chosen beyond question of need. Something possessed for its own qualities, because you want it near you, not necessarily to be used up but to be savored. The pleasure of excess. The love of what is not required. The appreciation of it for its own sake. For its excellence in relation to its own—what?—construction, fineness, superiority of material. How much beauty is enough, too much? How much pleasure?"[64]

If there were no others without money, if everyone had enough, then I think my struggle would be minimal. However, human life is intertwined. We are connected to each other. What I have is related to and affects what you have. As long as there are those without, I fear I will always wonder if what I have is enough or too much.

You may have heard of or read about Matilda and Bert who were visiting the Blue Hill Fair. As they were wandering about the exhibits of pigs, cows and Ferris wheels, they came across one of those open cockpit airplane rides with the advertisement: Ride for two—$10. Matilda said to Bert, "You know I sure would like to take one of those airplane rides." To which Bert replied, "I don't think so. Ten dollars is ten dollars." "But

Bert," Matilda said, "I'm seventy-two years old. I might never get a chance to fly in one of those planes." To which Bert replied, "I don't think so. Ten dollars is ten dollars."

At that point, the pilot, who was listening in on their conversation, said, "Tell you what folks. I'll take the two of you up for an airplane ride for nothin' as long as you don't say one word. But if you let out as much as just one peep, you owe me ten dollars." That sounded like a bargain they couldn't pass up, so Matilda and Bert climbed into the plane.

Well, that pilot did everything he could to get them to cry out. He did loop-de-loops, he did spins, he took the plane into steep dives. But neither Bert or Matilda said one word.

Defeated, the pilot finally brought the plane in for a landing and turned around to Matilda and said, "Well, I guess you got that plane ride for free. I did everything I could to get you to say something, but I didn't hear one word. To which Matilda replied, "It certainly was the ride of a life time and I was going to say something when Bert fell out of the plane...but ten dollars is ten dollars."

Matilda isn't the only one for whom "ten dollars is ten dollars." Money is so very important in our lives. As Lynn Twist, founder of the Hunger Project, puts it: "Our work is transformed into money. In my experience money is like water: When if flows freely it purifies, it creates growth; but when the flow slows or stagnates money becomes toxic and clouds our worldview. Depending on our attitudes and intentions, we can either get stuck as slaves to this process or be masters of it and keep money flowing where it can do the most work. That's where it gets its value. That's where it gets its soul."[65]

Money can do important work, and we can decide the work it can do. There are those we know who go without, who clearly do not have enough to eat, who struggle to pay the rent, their heating bills. There are others we know for whom those issues never cross their mind. Their struggle is to decide what to do with the money and resources they have. We are left with the question, "How do we do justly with what is ours?"

You and I are bombarded regularly with messages telling us we're not whole until we buy this or that car, or watch or perfume or the latest fashion. Another message that comes through newspapers, television, and billboards is that you are not sufficient. Something you buy will fix you, make you more complete. These messages too easily lead us to think from within a condition of scarcity—a mindset suggesting that no matter what we have or what is happening to us it is not enough. We are driven by these market forces to want more.

"I have a principle," writes Ms. Twist. "If we let go of what we're trying to get more of, that which we really don't need, it frees up reserves of vitality to make a difference with what we have. When you make a difference with what you have, it expands."

Until the day comes when there are no children being abused, when peace rules rather than war, when hunger is at no one's doorstep, when African-Americans are celebrated for the color of their skin, rather than scorned for it, when your community is a beacon for fair and affordable and integrated housing, when all marriages are honored and celebrated no matter what sexual orientation, then maybe you and I can stop asking what to do with our money. Until that day comes however, it is a question we must ask ourselves and each other, because money is the fuel to help us accomplish the holy work to which we are called.

What we do is something like Harriet's father, a trucker with an attitude, but a different kind of attitude. As he crisscrosses the country, he fills his truck with flowering bulbs and plants them along the highways upon which he travels, anonymously. "He was inaccessible and distant when I was young," Harriet says. "He thinks a lot about doing things for me and means to get in touch, but he never gets around to it. What pleases me is that this time he followed through. He expressed something of his own. Planting bulbs is *his*—not something someone asked for or forced him to do."

As she recounts the story to her boyfriend's mother, she adds, "I didn't see the beauty of his planting the bulbs, the giving part of it, till I casually mentioned it to you...and you were delighted, and you made me notice. I just took it for granted. That's the kind of thing he would do. He does have a soft side," she said wistfully. "Your noticing helps make his softer side apparent. ...I wonder how many other things he's done that I haven't noticed."

Now when Harriet sees daffodils and crocuses growing along a freeway she thinks of her dad and smiles. "Sometimes you need someone else's eyes to show you the beauty that's been in front of you all the time," she says.[66] That is what we're about. Helping the world be a bit better place. We do it together.

Novelist Anna Quindlen's advice comes to mind. "Get a life," she writes, "in which you notice the smell of salt water pushing itself on a breeze over Seaside Heights, a life in which you stop and watch how a red-tailed hawk circles over the water gap, or the way a baby scowls with concentration when she tries to pick up a Cheerio with her thumb and first finger.

"Get a life in which you are not alone. Find people you love, and who love you. And remember that love is not leisure, it is work. Each time you look at your diploma, remember that you are still a student, still learning how to best treasure your connection to others. Pick up the phone. Send an email. Write a letter. Kiss your Mom. Hug your Dad. Get a life in which you are generous. Look around at the azaleas in the...neighborhood where you grew up; look at a full moon hanging silver in a black, black sky on a cold night. And realize that life is the best thing ever, and that you have no business taking it for granted.

"Care so deeply about its goodness that you want to spread it around. Take money you would have spent on beers and give it to charity. Work in a soup kitchen. Be a big brother or sister. All of you want to do well. But if you do not do good, too, then doing well will never be enough. It is so easy to waste our lives: our days, our hours, our minutes. It is so easy to take for granted the color of the azaleas, the sheen of the limestone on Fifth Avenue, the color of our kids' eyes, the way the melody in a symphony rises and falls and disappears and rises again. It is so easy to exist instead of live.

"We may look back upon the present time, with its raucous shouts for 'more! more!' to have been the last gasp of the few in a world of limited resources and an expanding population. It is a useful, but demanding, art: doing more with less, and being able to say enough rather than more."[67]

The recipe for a sustainable society or a sustainable church or synagogue or mosque is to have people become known for what they allocate, what they invest in, rather than what they accumulate. Those people are about helping that culture or place of worship be what it is meant to be, where we care for each other in ways that enhance rather than destroy life.

I'm talking about a kind of prosperity where there is a sense of joy, creativity, and fulfillment in life. Wealth is truly understanding the beauty of a tree, it is being in love with a partner or the kind of work you do. Wealth is prosperity of the soul, the richness of a whole life, a complete sense of enough and not more.

There was once an old Jewish man. All he ever did in his spare time was go to the edge of the village and plant fig trees. People would ask him, "Why are you planting fig trees? You are going to die before you can eat any of the fruit that they produce." But he said, "I have spent so many happy hours sitting under fig trees and eating their fruit. Those trees were planted by others. Why shouldn't I make sure that others will know the enjoyment that I have had?"

I don't have a formula for what is right and wrong, for what is too much or not enough. But I have a guide: part of being human is to give back to others something of what we have received. I cannot always measure that in terms of money. It also means loving, and caring and generosity of spirit.

"To be a saint is to be human because we were created to be human, writes the Rev. Frederick Buechner. "To be a saint is to live with courage. To be a saint is to live not with the hands clenched to grasp, to strike, to hold tight to a life that is always slipping away the more tightly we hold it; but it is to live with hands stretched out both to give and to receive with gladness. To be a saint is to work and weep for the broken and suffering of the world, but it is also to be strangely light of heart in the knowledge that there is something greater than the world...it is to be a little out of one's mind, which is a very good thing to be a little out of from time to time." [68]

In Mary Gordon's novel, the character *B* asks, "Worth? What's worth?" That important question is answered differently by each of us. I confess that my worth is determined in part by how much I give away. I admit, however, knowing how much to give, how much to save, and how much to earn is a complicated question. I don't know how to decide what is right and wrong about money, about economic morality, about how much I should earn or how much I need. I know I want to become more fully human. Somehow that comes first. How I use my money reflects how fully human I am being.

Mary Ann Willis tells of giving her umbrella to a partially blind eighty-five-year-old woman who needed to get out from the rain. "I thought of it as my umbrella," she writes. "But as long as I thought of it as my umbrella that I was generously sharing, I was missing the point. It was an umbrella to be used as needed."

127

I don't think it is strange for her to think of her umbrella as hers. Most likely she paid for it, and even if it wasn't more than a $10 or $15 umbrella, it was hers. Most of us have a sense that the property we own is ours. Ms. Willis makes a leap, however. She suggests that her umbrella was to be used as needed, to be given away. "She needed it more than I did," Ms. Willis says.

What a different, strange sounding way to act. Yet are we not, in various ways, invited to share umbrellas? As Nancy Mairs puts it in her book, *Voice Lessons*, "The charity that begins here cannot rest here. It draws us over the threshold and off the porch and down the street on a journey out and out and out and out into the world which becomes our home, wherein charity continues until it becomes possible, in theory at least, to love the whole of creation with the same patience, affection, and amusement we first practiced in this place."

It is good to be people who search for answers, who welcome strangers as they are. Without such people and places there is no threshold from which to journey out and out and out into the world, where we humans are called to be with and for each other. Perhaps your place of worship or neighborhood or service club is just such a place. Hopefully, it is a threshold from which you share umbrellas, offering the same patience, affection, and amusement to the other in need.

Questions for further reflection

1. How do you answer the question, "What am I worth?" Can you measure your worth and if so how?
2. Does our desire to want more and do more positively or negatively impact our world? In what ways?
3. What is your relationship to money and its use? How much do you deserve?

The Three-Legged Stool

There is little difference between religion and science. Both are about the mystery of life. Religion is about: "Who am I?" "Where have I come from and where am I going?" "How should I live my life?" Science is about things scientific, theoretical, and problematical. Religion is about things scientific, theoretical, and problematical.

Religion informs science, and science informs religion. The two look at life—its meaning, its ways of being, its promises, and its possibilities. If you agree with the Rev. Dr. Forrest Church who says that religion is our response to having been born and the reality that we will die, then all is about science and religion and the two are ultimately about life. Reason and faith cannot be separated without diminishing our capacity to know ourselves, the world and the mystery that is beyond the answers with which we now live.

Religion is not about ignoring the facts; religion is living in the midst of scientific theory. Religion is about asking the questions, about discovery, about looking at what confronts us in life and our response. Does not science do something similar? To discover what is fundamental about life itself and how we uncover truth about life is what both science and religion ought to be about. However, what religion should bring to the table is a skepticism growing out of an ethical framework derived from a struggle to discover what makes life more fully human.

The Italian psychiatrist, Roberto Assagioli, tells a parable about interviewing three stonecutters building a cathedral in the fourteenth century. When he asks the first stonecutter what he is doing, the man replies with bitterness that he is cutting stones into blocks, a foot by a foot by three quarters of a foot. With frustration, he describes a life in which he has done this repeatedly, and will continue to do so until he dies. The second stonecutter is also cutting stones into blocks, a foot by a foot by three quarters of a foot, but he replies in a somewhat different way. With warmth, he tells the interviewer that he is earning a living for his beloved family; through this work his children have clothes and food to grow strong, he and his wife have a home, which they have filled with love. The third stonecutter gives the interviewer pause. In a joyous voice, he tells of the privilege of participating in the building of this great cathedral, so strong that it will stand as a holy lighthouse for a thousand years.[69]

The question to ask is what is it we are building; not who is to get credit, not how many bricks we have added, how much we have invested, but how wonderful the creation? Religion is the journey of creating a cathedral; not how much we spend making it, but what is celebrated in building it.

Once there was a three-storied universe, with an up, middle, and down. Then there was Copernicus who taught that the universe wasn't like that at all. Then there was a split with religious leaders saying that the world wasn't as Copernicus and Galileo said and scientists going right on saying yes it is, whether the pious and priestly like it or not.

There arose a place where science and technology live, the place of facts, of proofs, of information; and this place where religion, the sacred, the spiritual lives, the place of wonder, of mystery, of feeling. They became separate places, and our world divided the scientific and the technical from the spiritual or religious. That is to misunderstand science and religion. In their best moments both seek after the truth, not for credit but for bettering the humanity in us all.

We are not worse off because Copernicus discovered that we are not the center of the universe, that there is no up and down but mostly vast space. We are not worse off because Sir Ian Wilmut created two identical "cloned" sheep in his laboratory.

What I fear is that religious voices will try to do to science what the Vatican tried to do to Copernicus and Galileo: subdue it, control it, make it conform to a worldview no longer valid. There are religious voices that cry out against those who created synthetic sheep, but they also ask those same scientists to find the next anti-virus for HIV and the brain stimulant to stave off dementia, and to rebuke the ravages of heart disease. The same institute that created Dolly is testing the safety of another genetically created protein that may help those suffering from cystic fibrosis.

In genetic experiments, specially bred goats produce a protein that controls blood clotting. Clinical trials now going on will determine if this protein that looks just like the human version will help patients undergoing coronary bypass surgery and are vulnerable to clotting. Computers are reading patches of DNA on glass. Because these machines are a zillion times faster than anyone could ever read them, science may be on its way to a cure for many cancers.

Something more important to consider than whether science should push forward, is how are we to live with science that *will* push forward, in part because we will demand it and in part because research has a life of its own that will bring us both promises and dangers, hope and fear. Religion asks the same question. As the editorial writer for *The Economist* reminds us, "It is what people do that is good or bad, not what they can do." Science and religion, at their best, seek to find ways of doing what is most beneficial for all.

Human being is more a verb than a noun. We are works in progress, yet unfinished. Science and religion are places where we can advance or retard that progress. Research will continue, and the problems it will create are many. The answers are certainly not simple or clear. What is before us is how to find a place where science and religion meet.

There are many such places. Let me suggest one. In his book, *Imagined Worlds*, Freeman Dyson, professor of physics at Princeton and a pioneer in the area of low-grade nuclear physics, suggests that what concerns him is not that science will advance but that it will advance the needs of the rich and ignore those of the poor.

"The poorer half of humanity," he reminds us, "needs cheap housing, cheap health care, and cheap education, accessible to everybody, with high quality and high aesthetic standards." However, current technology continues along its present course, ignoring the needs of the poor and showering benefits upon the rich. He then concludes, "The widening gap between technology and human needs can only be filled by ethics."[70]

Dr. Dyson argues that the ethical debates, begun by the environmental movement, have put a stop to some of the evils created by technology and now must pressure those scientists to move on to produce the additional good that is needed. Not the free market by itself, but only expertise positively guided by moral principles will produce people-friendly technology.

Science has its home as does religion. At some place, however, they must meet, teaching each other. As the Rev. Ken Phifer writes: "How we act toward other people, especially those in need, is the surest sign of our worthiness and of our eventual fate." That may be the place where science and religion meet, meeting the needs of those in need.

The Hebrew Scriptures tell of Abraham who believed he was commanded by God to take his son Isaac into the wilderness and slay him as a sacrifice. At the last moment, as the father is about to plunge the knife into his child, a voice intervenes telling him to stop. What has always been troubling to me is how Abraham knew it was the voice of God and not Moloch, the Canaanite god of fire, to whom children were offered in sacrifice. Abraham had to assume the mantle of ultimate decision-maker. He had to decide the source of the command and in making the judgment he determined the value and the authority of the command. Only Abraham could conclude upon whose authority or voice he was acting and that he was making the right choice.

We are asked to decide, never having complete certainty. Therefore a certain humility and openness ought to be part of our way of being of use. Strong beliefs and opinions are good for they can guide and motivate us, but only as we remember that there are no final answers. There is only truth, for now that leads to other questions that call us to continue our search.

We call upon reason and faith for religious truth, both in our mind and the limits of the mind. While uncertainty remains, we trust that there is meaning in our existence. Reason and religion guide us, but certainty is not ours to give.

Our lives need peace, comfort and answers, yet we continue to question. There seems to be some fundamental drive for knowledge deep within us. Science, religion and the search for truth is a three-legged stool, each supporting us in the ultimate mystery that is life.

Questions for further reflection

1. Do science and religion differ? If so, how? Do they both discover the same truths or are they different ways of thinking about the world?
2. Are there ideas or beliefs about which we can have complete certainty? Is there ever a place for doubt? If so, where, when?

To Hold Fragile in Our Hands

A number of years ago I went to the Farmer's Market in Detroit looking for food for dinner. I asked one of the sellers if anyone there sold chicken and was told there were none there, but across the street there was a market where I could find many. So I went. When I arrived, I found a room filled with squawking, clucking chickens running about. When I spoke to the owner of my mission, he simply said, "Just point to the one you want and it's yours."

I confess that when I was asked to be the executioner, the whole idea of having been selected as the slayer meant chicken for supper did not appeal to me for a single moment. I left without dinner in hand.

Lee Goodman is a commercial fisherman who had occasion to realize our connection to other creatures not completely unlike ourselves. Occasionally a sea lion will move along his net a safe distance away, stopping now and then to grab a fish, flipping it into the air, as would a circus lion. "I holler from the bow," he writes, "[my] arms flailing, as fish after fish is taken from the net like bills expertly picked from my pocket. In the net I find half a fish, or just a head, or gill covers, or sometimes just silvery sequin scales marking where a fish went from mine to not mine."[71]

Mr. Goodman then notes how he has lost plenty of fish to sea lions, but also to competing fishermen and to the biologists who open and close the fishery where he sells his catch. One stocky, crewman offered, "Sea lions: All they need is a little vitamin L, in the diet." By which he meant lead from a bullet.

On a still morning in early July, this veteran of many years at sea discovered a baby otter drowned in his net. He describes pulling the otter across the gunwale of his ship, still tangled in the web. He had never caught a mammal before. "In my hands the tiny body felt surprisingly heavy and solid, complex and intricate. I could feel bones and strong muscles. It felt the way my children feel when I lift them sleeping from the couch and they curl in to me without waking."

He freed the dead otter and then went back to pulling his nets, but with a much more somber tone than before.

Later that month, while retrieving nets he had set the day before, a dead sea lion floated past his boat. He and his crew tied the lion to an anchor and called a fish and wildlife scientist who asked that he cut off its head and bring it to the laboratory in town.

"I measured its length," he writes, "and rolled it over and found a gunshot wound it its shoulder. It was a tiny hole, smaller around than a pencil."

It is easy for me to argue with those fishermen who would shoot a defenseless sea lion. They are an endangered species; they are beautiful, fun loving animals, who survive by eating fish from the sea and sometimes from fish caught in a fisherman's net. How could anyone justify shooting such a creature?

I am, however, a fish-eating mammal. I regularly go to the meat counter at my local grocery and order up a pound or so of the catch of the day. I count on those fishermen to bring me dinner, and I find it much more complicated to criticize their actions when I regularly benefit from them. In their way, by destroying these sea creatures they detest, they are protecting their jobs, they are making possible the food they bring to our tables, they are deciding for me what to kill.

There are things I find easy to describe as evil: the wars in Iraq and Afghanistan, the stealing of absentee votes, the bombing of abortion clinics, the low wages paid to those who clean hospital floors, care for the elderly, and serve us food. I also know that there are those who would see these things not as evil at all, but the very act of goodness; those who go to war are building a better tomorrow for a country that suffered from brutal dictatorship, some are stopping ineligible voters from going to the ballot box, others are saving the lives of innocent fetuses, and still others are providing jobs to workers and in a way that allows medical services to be offered to those in need.

We, however, are asked to make decisions about right and wrong, good and evil, just and unjust when all the facts aren't in. We make decisions when, if allowed, history might give us more information that might convince us to do otherwise.

As I listen to myself, evil has a powerful tone; it feels like a word that describes only the most vile and utmost of wrongdoing, but I wonder if this is not my way of adjusting. I wonder if I don't magnify the definition of this word so that it only includes extreme violations of human rights, and therefore by comparison my missteps don't measure up to anything worth noting. I suspect using the word evil more often to describe my errant behavior would help me pay more attention to the decisions I make.

I suspect we all have asked ourselves more than once: what could I have done differently? How could I have lived in such a way to prevent the evil I created? If only I had…? Each of us has our own list of regrets, of painful memories, of the wrongs we have done.

In New York City, housing is at a premium, rents are huge (except where controls are in place), and many developers convert transient hotels into luxury apartment buildings. Owners of these seedy residential hotels have taken to intimidating, threatening, and illegally evicting their tenants—most of them nonwhite, all of them poor—so that the buildings can be converted into co-ops and sold at a huge profit. Harry Stein describes the dilemma faced by a friend, Eric, who was considering buying an apartment in one of these converted hotels. "Look," Eric said, "I feel terrible about what happened to those people. I wish them justice. But why should I suffer? Someone's going to live in that apartment; why shouldn't it be me?"

Self-justification may be perhaps the original human reflex; most of us caught up in the syndrome of censure and reward at least want to appear to be doing the right thing, yet we adjust, we learn that to survive in this society is to tolerate in oneself a certain degree of inconsistency. As Mr. Stein puts it, "Every time we go to the supermarket, every time we deposit money in a bank, every time we let our kids watch some garbage on TV, chances are reasonably good that we're violating some belief or other."

As for his friend Eric, after some serious soul-searching, he transformed his understanding about buying the apartment and elected to keep hunting for a different place to live.[72]

Let us consider that evil is not a fallen state, but part of living in a state of becoming. As I look at the complexity of evolution, it seems plausible, in fact, much more realistic to assume that humanity is evolving ethically just as it evolved physically. Such development suggests that as we are physically maturing we are also moving toward the good; we are finding our way. Perhaps we are creating a Garden of Eden in some future time. We are part of that becoming, and our acts of evil are missteps on a continuum that is ongoing. As history continues humanity increases in wisdom and understanding. That may be hard to see amid the wars, the violence, the political incorrectness, the racism we see among us, but I suggest that evil is a condition of our lives and occurs because we are not yet fully conscious or whole. We are only part of a creation that is in process of becoming. Our missteps can be, if we learn from them, progress on the way to becoming fully whole.

As Dr. John Haught reminds us, "Evolution...means that the world is unfinished. But if it is unfinished, then we cannot justifiably expect it yet to be perfect. It inevitably has a dark side."[73]

Our lives are incomplete, and our understanding is incomplete. We are finding our way. In our search we will not get all things right. Rather we will make steps toward the good as we learn from what we have done wrong. That is not evil, that is not sin; it is living life in our unfinished state. I do not mean to minimize the wrong we do, or to condone the pain and suffering many inflict on others. I simply remind us that we are on a journey toward wholeness; making missteps is part of finding our way.

I return to Mr. Goodman and his life at sea, who writes, "It is winter now, and I still remember the solid and intricate weight of the baby otter. I remember the lion's liquid eyes and the distant operatic song and I feel the loss of these things. I worry that in the diesel-fuel sheen left by boats in our bay, and in the exhaust-yellow haze left by cruise ships in the fjords, more will be lost. With these losses comes a feeling beyond logic, a feeling that is innate, built into our cells, which relate to every other cell in every other thing that lives and ever lived and ever will. I'd like to protect things, to hold fragile things and feel in them the good solid weight of life," he concludes. "I wish I could hold them all the way I hold my son. All of Prince William Sound. All the world."[74]

The fisherman, Mr. Goodman, can't hold onto all things and he will even contribute to the losses he deplores, but he will also live by seeking to hold all the world in his caring hands, and I trust he will come to know that that is enough.

Today, I still pick out a chicken, turkey, or hamburger from the meat counter at the local supermarket, but I realize the hypocrite I am. I'm happy for someone else to do the killing on my behalf, but could not bring myself to do it alone. I try, however, to have my hands open wide where there is need for them.

Questions for further reflection

1. As we look out on the world do we see improvement in humanity's ethical behavior or do we still act in ways that indicate we have not progressed ethically much at all?
2. How should fisherman Goodman feel about killing that baby otter in his fishing net? Is he not simply working to provide a living for himself and others and, if so, should he be concerned about killing sea creatures that are hindering his ability to survive?

With a Thinking Heart

It has been close to twenty-five years since the space shuttle Challenger exploded seventy-three seconds after liftoff, killing all seven crewmembers aboard. You may recall those days just after the disaster, seeing pictures of the flames escaping from one side of the solid rocket booster. Eventually, the conclusion was that a leak from one of the rubber rings that seals the joint of the booster had allowed fuel to escape and burn, which in turn caused the explosion.

It took months to verify that conclusion, yet the problems with the leaks in those O-rings had plagued nine out of ten shuttle flights before Challenger, and such information had been widely known by the manufacturer, Morton Thiokol, and the National Aeronautics and Space Administration (NASA) years before the fatal crash.

Roger Boisjoly worked for Morton Thiokol and NASA for twenty years as an O-ring specialist. The night before the Challenger launch, he warned NASA officials that the O-rings always fail at 25 degrees and below, and because the temperature at launch time was predicted to be 18 degrees, he and others advised NASA to cancel the flight.

After the explosion, when they announced their reasons for opposing the lift-off, Boisjoly and another Morton Thiokol engineer Allan McDonald were demoted for their efforts to set the record straight by pointing out how the O-ring problem had been there for years. Although later reinstated, they and other colleagues who supported them were ridiculed and ostracized by fellow workers. One employee went to one of Boisjoly's supporters and said, "You SOB, you're trying to ruin the company. If you do, I'm gonna dump my kids on your doorstep."

The O-ring was redesigned, but according to Boisjoly, the redesigned equipment is just as susceptible to leaks as the original. "If those with information don't bring it forth," Boisjoly said, "how are you ever going to stop accidents from occurring again? I am not a loose cannon trying to get even with anybody. ...Say somebody's approaching a cliff, would you whisper or would you scream?"

That is the sound of a whistleblower: someone who screams when she or he sees the need, with the hope that the wrong will be made right.

Colonialist Thomas Paine was ridiculed and scorned for his pamphlet *Common Sense*, which now stands as one of the formative documents regarding the nature of God. The Rev. Theodore Parker, spoke out against slavery, only to find his parishioners and fellow clergy walking to the other side of the street when they saw him coming. Much earlier, Francis David, in 1568, argued before King Sigismund of Transylvania, that "faith is the gift of God," and there is no one particular brand of religious truth. It was that king who issued the first edict of religious toleration in European history, but when he died, David was imprisoned where he later died for continuing to stand by his religious views.

In another religious tradition, Etty Hillesum has written moving descriptions of her life in a Nazi concentration camp. One entry in her diary reads: "There is no hidden poet in me. Just a little piece of God that might grow into poetry. And a camp needs a poet, one who experiences life there, even there, as a bard is able to sing it. ...Let me be the thinking heart of these barracks."

Like Ms. Hillesum, we are to be the thinking hearts of our community—because, in part, the joy of life is found in the struggle to make wrongs right.

I often ask myself, however, in the vast scheme of things, in the fleeting time we are here, in the jungle of dog-eat-dog, why do we bother to affirm the right of conscience?

We do it because we can do no other.

For whatever reason we are here, be it because of our genes, or thoughtful parents, a wonderful teacher, a book we read, or a creator God, we care because it is in accord with our innermost self.

There was a wonderful series on television a few years back called *China Beach*, portraying medics and soldiers in Vietnam. In one episode, a doctor is trying to explain to one of the nurses just why he continues to work in such a dreadful place, with so little seeming reward. "You don't do it to make a difference," he says, "but you do it because it is right for you. Maybe that is the best we can hope. Not that our acts will obviously make a difference, but we act anyway because it is right for us."

People with thinking hearts live in accord with what their inner nature tells them and what they ought to do. That may mean they will be whistle blowers in a community that would have them make no noise at all.

The writer and naturalist Loren Eiseley describes an experience you may have heard before. It was an experience he had that speaks to what it means to have a thinking heart. "In the wee morning hours, the beach at Costabel is strewn with what the last high tide had left behind," Eiseley writes. "A hermit crab fumbling for a new home in the depths is tossed ashore... even torn fragments of green sponge yield bits of scrambling life striving to return to the great mother that has nourished and protected them.

"In the end the sea rejects its offspring. They cannot fight their way home through the surf which casts them repeatedly back upon the shore."

Tourists and professional shellers, eager to collect such treasures that are left behind the retreating tide, scramble before sunup to gather bags full of living shells. On one such morning, Dr. Eiseley set out for a walk amid these treasure hunters. As the sun begins to creep over the edge of the sea, he spotted a young man who every so often stoops down and picks up something and flings it into the sea. Eiseley walks over as the man reaches down for a starfish that was thrusting itself out of the stifling mud.

"It's alive," Eiseley said.

"Yes," the man replied, and with that he picked up the star and flung it out into the sea. "It may live," he said, "if the off-shore pull is strong enough."

Eiseley didn't know what to say, and only asked if the man was a collector.

"Only like this," he replied. "And only for the living." At that he picked up another star and as he flung it out into the surf, he added, "The stars throw well. One can help them."

Eiseley, who some describe as "a melancholic," walks away, wondering what this experience is about. The star thrower, he concludes, is mad, a person whose acts are folly.

The odds are against us, Eiseley believes. There is an eternal struggle that confronts humanity. Science has brought us face to face with a world that is so vast and complex that we pale into insignificance, and we, like the Psalmist of old, ask the question, "Who are we?" That singer of songs stood on some mountaintop and looking to the starry sky asked, "Oh Lord, my Lord, when I look at thy heavens, the work of thy fingers, the moon and the stars which thou has established, what is man that thou are mindful of him?"

When we read of X-ray messages reporting on galaxies billions of light years away, we ask, "Who are we in a universe where distances are noted in millions and billions of light years, distances we cannot even begin to comprehend?"

Eiseley retreats to his room also pondering his finiteness amid all that his scientific forebears have taught him, all the while recalling the star thrower bending down and throwing.

Then he asks, is science right? Is the natural order of things all there is? Are we, like the ooze from which we spring, full of desolation and disillusion? Is life molded in a direction that is unstoppable? He asks, in language of the poet, what the Psalmist also asked, who am I in the midst of all this?

He begins to rummage around in the attic of his house where he discovers an antique, shabby satchel that included a pile of old photographs and a tuft of hair bundled together, tied with a string and a note attached that read, "The satchel belongs to my son, Loren Eiseley." The "rat" of hair belonged to his mother and the portraits were of his ancestors, bearded men and heavily clothed women. And a picture of his mother. He sees himself as part of a larger picture.

The next morning Eiseley goes back to the beach. He seeks the star thrower. When he finds him, he silently picks up a still-living star and throws it out into the waves. "Call me another thrower," he says. And then he adds to himself: "He is not alone any longer. After us there will be others. ...I looked back across my shoulder...the star thrower stooped and flung once more. I never looked again. The task we had assumed was too immense for gazing. I flung and flung again while all about us roared the insatiable waters of death. I set my shoulders and cast, as the star thrower cast, slowly, deliberately and well. The task was not to be assumed lightly, for it was humanity as well as starfish that we sought to save...

"In some primordial time a fish-like creature climbed out of the ooze and slime breathing air. Clumsily it found its way on land, and in its struggle for survival set in motion the lineage that came to be in a star thrower, who loved not only himself but life. Somehow our ancestors sensed intuitively that we cannot exist without being hurlers of stars, and while we sometimes walk in pain and desolation, we do not walk in despair."

Eiseley concludes with these words: "Tomorrow I would walk in the storm. I would walk against the shell collectors and the flames. I would walk with the knowledge of the discontinuities of the unexpected universe. ...I would walk knowing of the rift revealed by the thrower, a hint that there looms, inexplicably, in nature something above the role men give her. I knew it from the man at the foot of the rainbow, the starfish thrower on the beaches of Costabel."[75]

Alone we don't amount to much...at least not in the grand scheme of things. We're pretty insignificant as far as what individuals can do. Yet ascribing to what we believe is the truth and trying to live by those truths is like that star thrower and the whistle-blowers who call out injustice and wrong—those who go against the odds, or scream when she or he sees the need, with the hope that the wrong will be made right.

We hurl our faith and compassion against a world hell-bent on destruction. Our answer to the Psalmist is that we throw ourselves out there, not just for the heck of it, but because it is of our nature. We can do no else. Like the star thrower must have said, "What I do may not seem like much, but that starfish I just tossed back to life sure thinks so."

Questions for further reflection

1. Can you name a few who are the conscience of your community? Do you offer words of right and wrong when you see injustice around?
2. How do you measure your worth? Is it of any value at all? If so, how?

What Hopes

Nine-year-old Frederic Hudson spent his Tuesday walking, talking, and playing like he had most every other day of his young life. Wednesday morning he awoke unable to move any part of his body except his eyes. His muscles were frozen, he had no voice, and he could only stare up. Whatever part of him he tried to move he couldn't. His jaw was frozen, his neck rigid as a rock. His breathing was short and panicked, and the pain was everywhere. He had contracted polio. It was 1943 and Jonas Salk had yet to make real his magic vaccine. There was no prevention and no medicine to work a cure.

Frederic's parents, who were struggling in the aftermath of the Depression and in the midst of World War II, drove him to the hospital. Frederic feared he was going to die. He remembers being placed on a very hard hospital bed, and hot packs that smelled like wet, burnt wool were applied over much of his body. They scorched his skin. For months, this was to be his treatment.

Into his hospital life Susan arrived, a quiet and caring nurse. Over the course of the next weeks and months, she was regularly at Frederic's side, while he remained in this rigid state. Over and over she repeated in one way or another, "Frederic, your future is hidden on the ceiling and you are the only one who can find it. Look for what you will be doing as you grow up. It's all up there. Will you be a track star, a tennis player, a scientist? Will you be going on trips to faraway places? Will you be going to summer camps and swimming? Will you go to college and become someone special? Will you marry and have a family? Frederic, all you have to do is study the ceiling. When you see your future it will start to happen."

I cannot imagine what it must have been like for Frederic, who could not bend even his little finger or move his mouth, to think about his future, to make plans to swing a tennis racquet or run a mile, let alone even walk down the street. All he could do was spend his days, weeks, months staring at a cracked, dirty ceiling above his immobile bed that cradled his immobile body.

Through her repeated encouragement, Susan convinced him that if he would keep rehearsing his vision on the ceiling sooner or later his body would begin to move again. "I trusted her to coach me toward my highest self," Frederic writes. "Knowing my eyeballs were my only moving part, she brought a projector into my room and flashed stories and pictures on the ceiling for me to consider as I pondered my future." Susan projected a checkerboard on the ceiling, and Frederic learned how to play chess alone. He also learned complex math, French, philosophy, and English literature. Because Frederic had said he dreamed of becoming a physician, she even brought him journals from Harvard, Yale, and Columbia's medical schools to help him plan his future.

Frederic admits that before he went into the hospital he wasn't a very good student. Imagine what it was like to work on fractions and multiplication tables, to read of Moby Dick and Silas Marner, and to think about med school when you cannot begin to feed yourself or get yourself out of bed. It must have been a Herculean task.

One day, while he was entranced by what he was envisioning on this now all too familiar ceiling he felt a wiggle in the toes of his left foot. It was only a little, but Susan advised him that this was the beginning of his unfolding future, not just getting well, but the realization of his dreams.

"You are now in training," she said, "so practice moving your foot for the rest of the month." She fastened a string to his toes and laced it up through an eyelet that she had screwed into the ceiling and tied a bell to it. "Ring the bell," she instructed him, as a way for him to reinforce what he was beginning to be able to do.

After success with his toes, Susan placed twine around his foot and threaded it through another pulley on the ceiling then attached it to a window. "Make the window go open and closed until it makes so much noise you'll bother the nurses," she instructed him. At the first bang the nurses came running. Only later did he learn that Susan had asked them to complain loudly about all the noise.

His room became a gymnasium, with ropes and pulleys everywhere. He came to call it his secret garden and became so fond of it he hated to leave, but leave he did. He gained almost complete use of his body, except he still could not touch his chest with his chin. Dr. Hudson did not go on to get a medical degree but a Ph.D. in philosophy from Columbia University. From there he created a research institute in California that bears his name, the Hudson Institute of Santa Barbara.

In one of the most famous passages in the Christian scriptures, Paul writes in a letter to the Corinthians that three things are of utmost importance: love, faith, and hope. While he gives highest marks to love, I suggest that hope may be more life giving. Not as a kind of Pollyanna response that says things are grim, but that I will be fine no matter what, but rather that, while there is no guarantee, there is the possibility of something better.

"To hope means to be ready at every moment for that which is not yet born, and yet not become desperate if there is no birth in our lifetime," writes psychiatrist Eric Fromm. "Those whose hope is weak settle for comfort or for violence; those whose hope is strong see and cherish signs of new life and are ready every moment to help the birth of that which is ready to be born."[76]

In 1977, the Nobel Prize was given to the chemist, Ilya Prigogine for his answer to the question, "If entropy is the rule, why does life flourish?" In other words, if all things move toward death and decay, if darkness is so much a part of life, why is evolution in living systems related to progress and not to disintegration?

Dr. Prigogine discovered that living systems respond to disorder and decay with renewed life. Disorder, he said, can play a critical role in giving birth to new, higher forms of order. He coined the term "dissipative structures," which showed that dissipation didn't lead to the demise of a system, it was part of the process by which the system let go of its present form so that it could reemerge in a form better suited to the demands of the present environment. As things begin to decay, he said, they create new information. As the system becomes more aware of this new information disturbances arise to such a degree that the system in its current form falls apart, but rather than die, in most cases the system reconfigures itself at a higher level of complexity, better able to deal with the new environment.[77]

Dr. Prigogine's discovery was that disorder can be a source of order and that growth is found in the things we fear most—fluctuations, disturbances, imbalances. He is saying that these things need not be signs of an impending disorder that will destroy us. Instead, fluctuations are the primary source of creativity. That is another way of saying that the darkness or that which we don't understand, rather than being fearful places, can provide the potential for growth and innovation.

I know that for some darkness is all around them; it seems to be all they know. For many the darkness does not go away, but the very process of nature confirms that in spite of the darkness there is the possibility of light and hope. Light can come into the midst of the darkness and exist alongside it. Just as the seed emerges from the darkness of the soil, light coming into the darkness may be part of the mystery of life itself. The irony is that in the midst of the darkness, light is the hardest thing to believe in.

In his memoir, *Darkness Visible: A Memoir of Madness*, Pulitzer Prize winner William Styron describes the darkness that was much of his life, in spite of his success and talent as a writer of such books as *Sophie's Choice* and *Nat Turner's Rebellion*. Deep depression ruled most of his waking moments; a life of winter was his much of the time. Despair seemed to rule his days and nights. He wrote, "The pain is most closely connected to drowning or suffocations—but even these images are off the mark."[78] He came close to suicide. Nothing seemed to help. But on a bitterly cold evening he was bundled up in a blanket watching a television rerun of a movie in which a young actress who had been in one of his plays moved down the hallway of a music conservatory. Beyond the walls came a contralto voice and a sudden soaring passage from the Brahms *Alto Rhapsody*.

"The sound," writes Styron, "which like all music—indeed, like all pleasure—pierced my heart like a dagger, and in a flood of swift recollection I thought of all the joys the house had known; the children who had rushed through its rooms, the festivals, the love and work, the honestly earned slumber, the voices and the nimble commotion. ...All this I realized was more than I could ever abandon."[79]

For Styron it was remembrances of love and restful sleep and joyous celebrations flooding his mind that turned him away from the dark.

As in springtime, especially for those in northern climes the light does return, not automatically, but only after a winter of bitter cold and much searching and listening.

For Styron, it was Dante who came closest to describing his experience when he wrote:

In the middle of the journey of our life
I found myself in a dark wood,
For I had lost the right path.

But then Styron reminds us that Dante concludes with:

And so we came forth, and once again beheld the stars.

As the Rev. Dr. David Blanchard puts it: "I believe, as surely as I believe anything, that in this life, everything is possible. That is not to say that we will have everything we want, or need, or deserve, but that our souls, the most essential and real dimension of our being, are not confined by the restrictions of the past or the limits of the imagined future. Sometimes that means we live, simply, in hope and trust that the time of renewal, of rebirth, is yet to come. But that it will come if we are alive and aware and receptive. We have been created to be free. We have been created to know joy. We have been created to love. We were not made to be exiles."[80]

Life so very often presents us with darkness, with obstacles, and in the midst of this darkness only more pain seems probable. Yet, if we believe there is something other than this darkness, life can be rewarding and fulfilling. If we give up on hope, the darkness will remain.

Hope lives in our souls and is present sometimes only in the tiniest of measure; in the wiggle of a toe or the very still voice within to give us the strength to carry on. We are enough. We were not made to be exiles. Disorder can give birth to the new.

Questions for further reflection

1. Which do you find more life giving: hope or love?
2. Describe the darkest time in your life. How did you recover? Or if you have not recovered what keeps you from being whole again?

ABOUT THE AUTHOR

The Rev. Richard Venus holds master's degrees in counseling, journalism, and theology. As a journalist, he covered cops, cows, and crime at the Hillsdale Daily News. As a United Methodist, he served as a minister in Detroit's inner city and in surrounding suburbs. Since becoming a Unitarian Universalist minister, he has served churches in Michigan and Ohio. A recipient of two Unitarian Universalist Association's Best Sermon awards, he currently serves the First Universalist Church of New Madison and writes for both spiritual and secular audiences.

He is learning to play the mandolin and the ukulele, chairs the Ohio Religious Coalition for Reproductive Choice and for many years served on the Planned Parenthood Board of Southwest Ohio.

He is married to Marcia, has three children and five grandchildren.

NOTES

1. "Making Our Peace with the Past." G. Peter Fleck. Quest. January 1994. P. 1.
2. "Hanging Around Until We Catch On." Richard Gilbert. Unpublished sermon. January 7, 199 P. 1
3. ibid. P. 5.
4. "To Err is Human." The Medusa and the Snail. Lewis Thomas. Bantam Books, 1997. P. 30.
5. *"The Wonderful Mistake," The Medusa and the Snail.* Lewis Thomas. Bantam Books, 1997, Pp. 23 ff.
6. "Depth of character develops best after facing a few failures." Leonard Pitts. *Dayton Daily News.*
7. "Hanging Around . . ." Gilbert, ibid. P. 10.
8. John Shelby Spong. "Our Moral Breakdown," The Human Quest. May-June 1995, Pp. 12–13. As the Episcopal Bishop of the Dioceses of New Jersey, he has thought about this and suggests several reasons for this growing incivility.
9. "American Adam." Garry Wills. NY Review of Books, March 7, 1997. Pp. 30 ff.
10. ibid. P. 31.
11. "Tree of Failure." David Brooks. New York Times, January 14, 2011. P. A23.
12. "Riders Face a Beggar and Themselves," New York Times, Tuesday, December 9, 1997. P. D18.
13. For a helpful understanding of the changing views of money, time and work see Robert Wuthnow's Poor Richard's Principle, Princeton University Press, 1996. cf. Pp. 54 ff.

14. Wuthnow, ibid. P. 92.
15. Church, Forrest. Life Lines: Holding On (And Letting Go). Beacon Press, 1996. P. 168.
16. ibid. P. 169.
17. ibid. P. 171.
18. Wuthnow, P. 373.
19. "Does praying for a sick person's recovery help?" Malcolm Ritter. Dayton Daily News, March 31, 2006. P. 1.
20. "Despite study some still have faith in prayer." Springfield News Sun. April 4, 2006. P. 1 Sec. c.
21. There is another Psalmist who reminds me that a vengeful god is both misunderstood and difficult to understand.
22. Bozarth, Alle. Life Prayers from Around the World. Elizabeth Roberts/Elias Amidon, Eds. HarperCollins, 1996. Pp. xxii-xxiii.
23. Zinn, Howard. A People's History of the United States 1492–Present. Perennial Clasics, 2001. Pp. 1–2.
24. ibid. P. 8.
25. ibid. P. 21.
26. Bragg, Rick. All Over But the Shoutin'. Vintage Books, 1997. P. 55.
27. ibid. Pp. 246–7.
28. Much of the medical information in this discussion comes from Why We Hurt: The Natural History of Pain. Frank T. Vertosic, Jr. MD. Harcourt, Inc. 2000 Pp. 8–33.
29. I am indebted to my colleague Mark Morrison-Reed who wrote of death in similar terms in the UUA Meditation Manual Been In The Storm So Long. Skinner House Books, 1991. P. 41.
30. Spelman, Elizabeth V. Fruits of Sorrow: Framing Our Attention to Suffering. Beacon Press, 1997. P. 171.

31. For more on this topic, see "Against Vengeance." Rebecca Parker. UU World, Sept/October 2002. P. 15.

32. ibid. P. 16.

33. To read more of his thoughts, see The Meaning of It All. Ridhard P. Feynman. Helix Books, 1998.

34. For a detailed and fascinating description of the progress of evolution see Jared Diamond's book Guns, Germs, and Steel. W.W. Norton & Co., 1991.

35. "Waste Land: An Elegy." Mary Oliver. Orion. September/October 2003. Pp. 29 ff.

36. This is not his real name.

37. I am indebted to Daniel Callahan's, Setting Limits: Medical Goals In An Aging Society, for much of the content in this sermon.

38. "Getting to Yes, when the world keeps trying to say No." William P. Zelazny, Quest, CLF/July- August 1998, P. 2. Rev. Zelazny' article gave me several ideas for this chapter.

39. Thurman, Howard. Meditations of the Heart. Harper & Brothers, 1953. Pp. 52–3.

40. "The Flow of the River." Loren Eiseley, The Rhetoric of Yes, Ray Fabrizio, Edith Karas, Ruth Menmuir, editors. Holt, Rinehart and Winston, 1973. Pp. 20–21.

41. Zinn, Howard. You Can't Be Neutral on a Moving Train. Beacon Press, 1994. P. 208.

42. Quest, July-August 1998. ibid., P. 3.

43. Rotheiser, Ronald. The Holy Longing.

44. Much of this conversation is from an article in the Spring 2001 issue of Spirituality & Health. Pp. 33 ff.

45. Dillard, Annie. For the Time Being. Vintage Books, 1999. P. 170.

46. "England Battles Racism That Infests Soccer." George Vecsey. New York Times, Sunday, February 2, 2003. P. 1 Section 8.

47. Takaki, Ronald. A Different Mirror: A History of Multicultural America. Little, Brown, 1993. P. 12

48. "Malign Neglect." The New York Times, May 22, 2011. Opinion page 7.

49. Bell, Derick. Ethical Ambition. Bloomsbury, 2002. P. 177.

50. Gilligan, Carol. In a Different Voice. Harvard University Press, 1982, P. 17.

51. ibid. P. 21.

52. Singer, Irving. The Pursuit of Love. Johns Hopkins University Press. 1994. P. 176.

53. Lewis, Thomas, M.D., Fari Amini, M.D., Richard Lannon, M.D. A General Theory of Love. Vintage Books, 2001. See Pp. 76–80.

54. "September 11: The View from the West." Jonathan Raban. New York Review of Books, September 22, 2005. P. 6.

55. 48 Barber, Benjamin R. Jihad vs. McWorld. Random House, 1995.

56. ibid., P. 4

57. Stephen Jay Gould, I Have Landed: The End of a Beginning in Natural History. Harmony Books, 2002. Pp. 394-5.

58. Rabin. ibid. P. 8

59. Basic Books, 1995. P. 172.

60. Rebecca Parker. "Wake Up, Music in the Depths of my Soul." An unpublished sermon. July 14, 1996.

61. Nouwen, Henri J.M. Reaching Out. Image Books, 1975. Pp. 54 ff.

62. ibid. P. 96.

63. Alexander. ibid. P. 1.
64. Gordon, Mary. Spending: A Utopian Divertimento. Schribner, 1998. P. 74 f.
65. "The Soul of Money," Noetic Sciences Review, Autumn 1997. P. 23
66. Bender, Sue. Everyday Sacred. HarperCollins Publishers, 1996. P. 111.
67. McKeeman, Gordon B. Out of the Ordinary. Skinner House Books, 2002. P. 24.
68. Buechner, Frederick. The Magnificent Defeat. Harper and Row, 1966. Pp. 119–20.
69. Remen, Rachel. Kitchen Table Wisdom, Riverhead Books, 1996. P. 161.
70. Freeman Dyson. "Can Science Be Ethical?" New York Review of Books. April 10, 1997. P. 48.
71. "The Weight of Things." Lee Goodman. Orion Magazine. November-December 2004. P. 53.
72. "Between Good and Evil." Harry Stein. Ethics (and Other Liabilities). St. Martins Press, 1982. P. 117 ff.
73. ibid. P. 169
74. "Weight of Things". ibid. P. 55.
75. Eileley, Loren. The Star Thrower. HarcourtBraceJovanocich. New York, 1978. Pp. 169–185.
76. Marshall, Bruce. "Hope Vs. Optimism." The Quest. April 1993, P. 8.
77. Margaret J. Wheatley. Leadership and the New Science. J. Berrett-Koehler Pub., San Francisco, 1994. P. 19.
78. Styron, William. Darkness Visible: A Memoir of Madness. Random House, 1990. P 17.
79. ibid. Pp. 66-7
80. Blanchard, David. A Temporary State of Grace. Skinner House Books, 1997. Pp. 22–3.

Made in the USA
Charleston, SC
17 October 2011